How to Become the Neighborhood Millionaire

The Simplest Book Ever Written on Saving
Quickly, Retiring Early and Living Your Dream Life

David Madow

Praise for How to Become the Neighborhood Millionaire

"David Madow has the unique ability to bring out your inner strengths that will motivate you to be financially independent."

- Desmond Willoughby, Founder, BBD Jewelry, Queens, NY

"I read this book in one sitting and it will change my financial life forever."

- Evan Scott, Software Engineer, San Francisco, CA

"It doesn't take a 500-page book to teach the principles of becoming a millionaire and enjoying your ideal life. David Madow certainly hit a home run with this one!"

- Herb Runkle, Kenner, LA

"For the last thirty plus years Dr. David Madow has helped tens of thousands of dentists become more successful in their practices. With this book he will do the same for people's financial lives."

-    J. Tony Llera, DDS, Ft. Lauderdale, FL

"If you are in a 'financial funk,' this is the book for you!"

-    Steve Jensen, Ogden, UT

"I've known David Madow both professionally and personally for more than 25 years. I know of no one better to teach the many aspects of money, including how to make it, how to keep it, and most importantly, how to enjoy it. I've known Dave to consistently practice what he preaches. While enjoying great financial success, Dave chooses to spend his money on what will enrich his life. You don't have to be 'rich' to have a rich life!"

-    Dr. Michael Goldstein, Founder and CEO
of Goldstein Management, Williamson, GA

"There are many 'experts' out there creating an awful lot of noise. But if common sense, getting ahead and the ability to sleep at night are all important to you, there is only one voice to listen to. That voice is David Madow.

- Dr. Ron Levine, Rockville, MD

"David Madow truly practices and lives what he teaches, and is a great person to look to for financial and real life advice. In his book 'How to Become The Neighborhood Millionaire,' David creates an effective blueprint you can follow to achieve your best financial self."

- Dr. Jeff Labishak, Zanesville, OH

"I have found Dr. David Madow to be very knowledgeable to help me through some tough financial situations. He's the consummate professional! I highly recommend his new book 'How to Become the Neighborhood Millionaire'"

- Jan Stahl, Ellijay, GA

"This is the book that takes the mystery and the difficulty out of becoming a millionaire and retiring wealthy. Unfortunately most people are lost when it comes to personal finance. Most financial books are complicated and long. By the time the reader finishes he or she is more confused than ever. In 'How to Become the Neighborhood Millionaire' David Madow shares simple principles that he's been using for decades that will help anyone become financially independent."

- Dr. Mark Keiser, Baltimore, MD

"David Madow has been a mentor of mine for several years now. His no nonsense approach to finance and wealth building is a breath of fresh air. I'm a big supporter of investing early, staying consistent no matter what the market is doing, and also striving for financial education. Discussions with him have helped me fine tune my own wealth building strategies and help separate the signal from the noise when it comes to the financial arena."

- Eric Kough, Chesapeake, VA

"This book is sharp, smart, and to the point. Since David doesn't make his money from secrets, he's free to tell you the truth: Getting rich can be simple."

- Todd Brison, Dickson, TN

"David Madow offers world class financial and business advice. His insight is valuable whether you're flourishing or facing a tough time. There's no one else that I would trust more."

    -   Joshua Hall, Founder, Hall Physical Therapy, LLC, Salt Lake City, UT

ISBN: 978-0-578-87313-8 (Paperback)

Any references to historical events, real people, or real places are actually real. The author has done his best to cover up the sins of those who are most-definitely guilty of bad financial decisions. Seriously speaking though, in some instances, for confidentiality reasons, names and characteristics may have been changed.

This publication is designed to provide accurate and authoritative information in regard to the subject matter covered. It is sold with the understanding that the publisher is not engaged in rendering financial, legal, accounting, or other professional services. If you require legal advice or other expert assistance, you should seek the services of a professional.

Front and back cover designs by Ridzz.

First printing edition 2021.
David Madow/Peak Five Ventures LLC
358 S 700 E
Suite B-116
Salt Lake City, UT 84102

Website: www.davidmadow.com
Email: dave@davidmadow.com

To every single one of you who have crossed paths with me in the past, the present, or will do so in the future. This book is dedicated to you and your financial success, but even more importantly... your happiness!

Table of Contents

Introduction

Welcome. Are you tired of running in circles on your attempts to save and invest? Are you sick of drowning in jargon from so-called "experts?" Are you looking for real, simple advice for finally finding financial freedom?

If so, then congratulations! This is the exact book that will take you to your journey of becoming "The Neighborhood Millionaire."

Since you picked up this book, I'm guessing you're a bit like me. You aren't concerned with gold toilets and massive houses. You aren't looking for a fancy lifestyle. You aren't worried about driving flashy cars. You don't mind dressing in regular clothes. You have no need for buckets of jewelry or piles of diamonds. You never brag or talk about yourself.

You don't want to be rich, just comfortable. You long to live the quiet life of the Neighborhood Millionaire!

Imagine what that would feel like to continue a calm life among your family and friends... but to know deep down that:

- Whatever life throws your way, you'll be ready for it.

- Whenever emergencies try to shake you, you'll handle them with ease.

- Wherever you want to travel, you'll simply book tickets and go.

- Whoever follows in your footsteps will have a head start on their finances.

This book is the path to those freedoms.

Just by picking this book up, you have taken the first step to becoming the Neighborhood Millionaire! This is your path to waking up one morning with the true peace and comfort that comes with wealth without selling your soul, compromising your values, or flaunting your riches.

Who the heck am I to make such claims? Fair question.

I am a regular person, probably not much different than you. I am neither a financial planner, an economist, nor an accountant. I have never worked on Wall Street.

Instead, I am simply a student of money. I have researched the ins and outs of personal finance for most of my adult life. I have probably made every mistake you can possibly make[1] I have "walked the walk," and not just "talked the talk." Although I am not from Texas, I hear they have a name for those

---

[1] I'll certainly share these boneheaded moves so you don't have to suffer like me!

people: "Big hat, no cattle!" I never wanted to be one of those guys.

Even after all my mistakes, false starts and bumps in the road, I have still been able to accumulate enough of a nest egg that will provide me a comfortable living for the rest of my life. Let me tell you - that takes off a lot of pressure! It's hard to explainthe extent of that freedom.

Although I am certainly a capitalist, I am not writing this book to make money or to become a New York Times best-selling author[2]. I am doing so out of a driving passion to help people like you work smarter, not harder, and to be able to get rid of your financial stress and worries forever. By purchasing this book, you're not only learning the secrets for yourself, you're giving others a chance to do the same. Thank you for your generosity.

---

[2] Although I DEFINITELY wouldn't be upset if that happened.

I am hoping The Neighborhood Millionaire will become a cult classic, even if the cult is small. If my teachings only change just one person's life, I am happy. I hope that person turns out to be you.

> **Just by picking this book up, you have taken the first step to becoming the Neighborhood Millionaire.**

Because the financial advice market is so full of crazy teachers and false promises out there, most people are totally confused! I watch financial gurus talk about issues that only matter to a tiny percentage of the world and wonder - "Where is the practical advice?" "Where is the real education?" "Where is the road map for normal people like me?"

The lie told over and over is that financial success is reserved for a few geniuses. The truth is financial independence is simpler than you think.

In the pages that follow, you'll find the road map I was looking for on my journey to becoming a Neighborhood Millionaire. If you follow the advice in this book, you will never again be confused about how to thrive financially. As a bonus, you won't have to make all the stupid mistakes I did.

Here's my promise to you: this book will be no-nonsense. It will be easy to understand and enjoyable to read. I will spell everything out for you step by step. And maybe even tell you a few stories and jokes along the way.

By the end, you'll have the path to earning your place as a Neighborhood Millionaire.

This process will work for you no matter what stage of life you are in right now. Whether you are a college student, a graduate student, a plumber, a

factory worker, a doctor, an electrician, a retiree…
basically any person who needs oxygen… this book
can help you move to the next level financially.
Wherever you may be in your life's journey, it is
never too early or never too late to make money
work for you.

I want to be very clear. Being a millionaire itself
does not create or equal happiness. It does not make
you a better person. What it DOES give you is
freedom.

Freedom is the greatest gift you could hope for.

So let's try this. Before you turn the page, close your
eyes and say out loud:

"I am becoming The Neighborhood Millionaire."

The First Steps

Chapter 1 - Dare to Dream

Many financial books start out by diving straight into the math, the strategies, and the secret investing techniques. This is a mistake. If you don't build the foundation, you can never build a house. This road to becoming a Neighborhood Millionaire starts in your mind.

I want you to dream first. Dream about how your wealthy life could be. Look into your future. What do you see? Where do you live? Who is with you? How does it feel, taste, and sound? If you don't answer these questions, you won't have the resilience to follow any of the practical instructions that follow. Please, do not skip forward until you complete the exercise.

You have undoubtedly heard the old expression that goes something like "If you don't know where you want to go, you will likely never get there." This holds true with wealth.

Many people have vague ideas such as "I want to be rich," or "I just want to get rid of my money problems." These are mostly empty thoughts and do not mean anything, nor will they get you anywhere.

When you dream, make it clear. Make it real. Make it concrete.

Do you need a few examples of dreams? Here are some. See which ones, if any, resonate with you!

- I would like to work because I love it, not because I have to.
- I would like to retire young and live a modest life in a beach town.
- I want to live in the mountains and ski every day possible.
- I want to make tons of money and live luxuriously[3]

_____

[3] You might reconsider this one after finishing this book, though.

- I want to be debt free. I never want to owe another dime to anyone.
- I would like to work a nice job, live well below my means and save more money than I spend every single year.
- I would like to travel the country in an RV with my wife and cat.
- I would love to become a minimalist, with as few possessions as possible.
- I want to become the Neighborhood Millionaire!

Maybe all of these dreams are for you. Maybe none of them are. These examples serve to get you thinking. What type of life do you want to live? Spend as much time as it takes to create a dream you can wake up ready to go after.

Write these dreams down in a notebook. Make as many notes as you can about your ideal life. What does your dream look like?

Keep that notebook by your side and carry it with you. Whenever you're feeling tired and uninspired, read over your dream. Take yourself to the future. Fill yourself up with the air of freedom.

Once you've done that, turn the page, close your eyes and say out loud:

"I am becoming The Neighborhood Millionaire."

Chapter 2 - From Dreams to Goals

Congratulations for dreaming. It's one of the most powerful things you can do in life. Now, let's fine tune those dreams and turn them into goals.

What is the difference between a dream and a goal? A dream for your life is exactly like the one you have when you sleep... it's a bit vague. It's fuzzy. It's cloudy. It has a bad habit of being forgotten when you wake up and go back to the cold, hard reality of daily life.

If you truly want to become the Neighborhood Millionaire, dreams cannot stay dreams. You need to turn them into goals now. Goals make dreams more concrete. So that you don't get overburdened, let's start slow. Take your favorite dream and turn it into a goal.

For example... your dream might be something like:

"I want to be wealthy enough to retire while I still have great health."

The financial goal that enables your dream would be:

"I will have $3 million dollars in my investment portfolio when I turn 50 years old."

See the difference?

If you have four different dreams, you'd convert them all into goals. It's not important that you be super accurate right now. What is important is that you start to translate those vague, dreamy terms into tangible, real steps. "I live a life of luxury" might become "I make $75,000 in monthly passive income." A dream of "travelling as much as I want to" might turn into "I work a job that makes me $100,000 per year and gives me a completely flexible schedule."

Fair warning: your brain will try to figure out how to accomplish these goals immediately. Silence that voice. The how comes later. The WOW comes now.

As a reminder, be sure to select your dreams and goals carefully. I'd rather you chase after a small personal goal than a huge one you don't care about so much. "I want to be very wealthy" is a dream. It's not good or bad, right or wrong. It's just a dream. While you're turning that dream into goals, though, be sure they are goals you really want.

When I was younger, I was making a decent amount of money as a dentist and as a second business owner. And with that came the large house, the nice clothes for the wife, the expensive travel, toys, private schools for the kids… the list goes on and on.

These days I live a minimalist lifestyle. I travel around the country in an RV seeing the beauty of America with my wife, Yoko. We live in a place where we can ski, hike, mountain bike, and stand up paddle board any time we want (depending on the weather of course)! I feel no need to accumulate things or impress anyone.

My first wife and I parted ways many years ago, and I am now with a woman who I am much more in alignment with financially and philosophically. We chase the simple pleasures in life.

Although skiing, hiking, camping, biking and running are wonderful, they aren't fulfilling on their own. I mix in some work as well. The difference now is I no longer work because I have to. That is the best feeling in the whole wide world. I could literally goof off every day for the rest of my life and my bills would be paid with the money I have accumulated.

Writing this book, although it is considered "work," is really a lot of fun. Why? Because with every paragraph I complete, I am reminded of how many people's lives I will be changing for the better once. I am literally thinking of YOU right at this moment, saying something like "I am so happy to have this information. I wish I would have known this stuff forty years ago!"

Since I have done it many ways, I will tell you early on in this book that the most peace I have ever had in my life is right now. I live way below my means, I invest what I don't spend, and I do what I love as often as possible.

For me, there is no better life than this. I stay very low key, under the radar, it does not cost very much and my financial worries are all but gone. Remember this as you change your dreams to goals - no financial worries equal freedom. That's the Neighborhood Millionaire's mantra.

> **I no longer work because I have to. That is the best feeling in the whole wide world.**

Don't forget to keep your notebook full of dreams and goals handy. You need to ALWAYS be looking at it, thinking, dreaming and modifying as needed. You should read these goals every day or at least several times per week.

Personally, I look at my goals almost every day. Once a year (normally on New Year's Eve), my wife and I get together for a nice dinner[4]. We have what we call a "board meeting" to review and update our goals. I highly recommend you do the same once you're finished with this process[5].

Now, before you turn the page, close your eyes and say out loud:

"I am becoming The Neighborhood Millionaire."

---

[4] By the way, a "nice dinner" to us is not necessarily an expensive dinner. It's generally a cool little ethnic restaurant that is not noisy where we can enjoy good food and get work done!

[5] If you ever need help defining your goals, or just want to share them for some affirmation, I would love to hear from you. Feel free to email me at dave@davidmadow.com

Chapter 3 - Determine Your Net Worth

You've got your dreams and you're goals. Now, we'll move into the practical steps of becoming a Neighborhood Millionaire, start at the very beginning (a very good place to start!)

What EXACTLY is a millionaire? Most people do not truly understand what it means to be a millionaire. One reason for this is the huge amount of misinformation circling around.

First off, a millionaire is *not* someone who earns a million dollars a year. A millionaire is *not* someone who has a million dollars in investments. A millionaire is *not* someone who has a million dollars of cash sitting in the bank.

Here's what a millionaire is:

A millionaire is a person who has a net worth of one million dollars or more.

That means in order to determine how close you are to Neighborhood Millionaire status, you must know your net worth. What exactly is your net worth? Great question. Your net worth is defined as your assets minus your liabilities. When that number reaches a million dollars, you are officially a millionaire.

It's as simple as that!

In order to reach any destination, you first need to know where you're starting. Grab a pen and paper. Let's figure out your net worth right now.

On the left side of your page, write down every **asset** you own, as well as its financial worth. An asset is anything you own that has value. This includes money in the bank, investments, the market value of your house, business interests, cash in your safe… everything[6].

---

[6] Well, *almost* everything. When computing my net worth, I do not include things like my vehicles, furniture, computers,

Okay got them all down? Add up the numbers and write the total at the bottom of the page.

After the first step, your page should look something like this:

```
  $20,822 = Bank Account
  $76,320 = Investments
  $105,000 = House Value
+ $1,400 = Cash & Jewelry
──────────────────────────
  $203,542 = Assets
```

Now let's figure out your **liabilities**. This would be anything you owe. Your mortgage balance, HELOC, personal loans, student loans, car loans, credit card balances, medical bills, and of course the money you

────────────────────────────

phones, etc. It's not necessarily wrong to do that, but the numbers usually aren't enough to matter.

still owe old Uncle Wilbur! Do not leave out anything[7].

Just like with the assets, write down the dollar amount next to the item.

After the second step, your page should look something like this:

```
     $6,258 = Credit Card
    $17,500 = Personal Loan
    $16,517 = Car Loan
 +  $95,215 = Mortgage
   ─────────────────────
   $135,490 = Liabilities
```

The final step is to subtract your liabilities from your assets. That part should be pretty easy. The number you come up with is your net worth. Subtract that number from one million, and you'll be left with the amount needed to become a millionaire.

---

[7] By the way, expenses such as groceries or the electric bill are not liabilities.

Here's what the final result of your net worth calculation will look like:

$$\$203,542 = \text{Assets}$$
$$- \$135,490 = \text{Liabilities}$$
$$\overline{\$65,052 = \text{Net Worth}}$$

You will now have one of three reactions. The first possible reaction is a twisting, uncomfortable stab in your stomach. It is very possible for your net worth to be zero or even negative. If you have more liabilities than assets, yours is negative. This is actually pretty common.

The second possible reaction is a shrug. Maybe you're doing better than you thought. You've been able to avoid big debts early in life, and you're likely looking at a home loan, a few credit cards, and maybe a car payment. Your net worth might be positive, even though you don't feel that great about it.

The third possibility is relief. Although this is sadly rare in America these days, you might be looking at a net worth of several hundred thousand dollars or more. That means you've probably steered clear of silly decisions or big mistakes. Congratulations! If you've done that without a book like this, you've done well.

What's important is that no matter where you are right now, it only takes one decision to start a whole new direction in life. Don't give up. Don't give in. Don't despair. No matter how far away you are from millionaire status, you can do this!

Now, before you turn the page, close your eyes and say out loud:

"I am becoming The Neighborhood Millionaire."

Chapter 4 - How NOT to Become a Neighborhood Millionaire

Let me guess. You calculated your net worth, and then you immediately thought:

"Okay... now I'm going to start working my butt off to make some SERIOUS money."

That's good! It's a useful, motivational thought.

However, it's also too narrow. Overemphasizing your focus on income can leave you not only broke, but broken. I have seen too many people earn more and more each year, and then wake up a decade later, trapped and poor. Imagine earning over six figures and still feeling like you have no money! It happens all the time.

Many years ago I had a doctor friend who had the so-called "perfect life." Let's call him Paul. Dr. Paul had a lovely wife, two wonderful girls, a nice home in Baltimore County's Worthington Valley with a swimming pool, a hot tub in the backyard and two beautiful late-model cars in the garage. Paul went golfing every weekend with his high-class neighborhood buddies, paying to play at all the exclusive courses around town. Everything looked good from the outside.

Unfortunately his doctor's salary was not quite enough to maintain this charming lifestyle.

Paul would always say to me, "David, if I could just make another $30,000 per year, I'd be set and never have any money problems."

You know what? Back then I was naive enough to believe that was true.

Paul fell victim to one of the biggest lies in personal finance. "If I only had _____ more money, everything would be fine." Pardon my language, but I call bullshit on that. How else could big celebrities like Johnny Depp make more money than God and then end flat broke??

Please listen very closely to what I am about to say. It is the pearl of wisdom that trumps all of the others. If you aren't willing to accept this, go grab another book.

Spend less money than you make. Always. No exceptions. Start now.

This is called "living below your means," and it is a core principle of Neighborhood Millionaires. Few people follow this principle. Do you know why? Because these days, people feel that they "deserve" certain things no matter how much or how little money they have.

My neighbor Chris said to me the other day "I deserve that leased $40,000 SUV in my driveway because it's got all of the safety features, and we have three kids we need to transport. The comfort and safety of my family is paramount."

The problem is, Chris is making $55,000 per year and has some credit card debt. Someone making $55,000 per year has no business having a leased $40,000 vehicle sitting in the driveway. It makes no financial sense at all, regardless of how good his monthly payments[8] may seem.

Now before you crucify me, there is nothing "wrong" with making $55,000 per year. Or $25,000 per year. Or $100,000 per year. I know some millionaires who are real a-holes and some who are the kindest people you'd ever want to meet and hang out with. The amount of money you make does not define you. It does not make you a good person or a bad person.

But there is objectively, something wrong with living above your means, even by a little bit. It's so easy to justify an extra purchase here and there. Over time,

---

[8] Many people lose their chance at wealth on seemingly cheap monthly payments. We will talk about this in depth later in the book.

though, those extra purchases can cause your entire future to spiral away.

Keep that in mind as we move forward.

Now, before you turn the page, close your eyes and say out loud:

"I am becoming The Neighborhood Millionaire."

Spend less money than you make. Always. No exceptions. Start now.

Chapter 5 - The True Cost of Living Above Your Means

I know, I know. You read the last chapter, which means that you have accepted living below your means... for now.

But what happens in a month's time, when this book is tucked away safely on your shelf? How strong will you be then? Businesses are armed with every trick in the book to separate you from your hard-earned cash. It's a jungle out there, so let me drive this idea of living below your means deeply into your brain.

Let's say you have a family income of $6,000 per month. You decide that you "deserve" some more expensive things that will make your expenditures $6,500 per month. Can you buy that thing even if you don't have the cash? Of course!

You can't just walk into the store and say "I want this but I do not have the money this month," though. The salesperson will tell you to take a hike. So you borrow the money from somewhere. How do you do it? There are various ways, but the most common is you simply pull out your credit card. You make the purchase, leave the store and you probably feel great! Simple.

Here's the problem. That borrowed money is not free. There is a price that you will have to pay later, and it's a big one. It's called debt.

In essence you are borrowing against something in the future. It must be paid back. Sometime. Somehow. What you tell yourself is that you'll cut your spending next month and pay off the balance.

That almost never happens. Next month is a little tight because you will still have all your previous recurring expenses. You decide to make the minimum payment on your credit card. You make a partial payment. You'll get it all off... eventually.

You have just entered a very dangerous world called the "Debt Spiral."

If you go over budget in a month (even by a slight amount) the new debt gets added to your previous balance. Add in the ridiculously high monthly interest that you will be paying[9] and the debt spiral gets worse. Pay the bill even a day late, and more astronomical charges will start to accrue.

The early signs of this disaster are often ignored. Why? Because a new credit card is often easier to get than a gallon of milk. You keep buying. If you need more available funds, you get another line of credit. You put just a "little bit" on each card. It will be easy to pay them off when you get a little extra cash. And surely you'll get extra cash soon.

Right?

---

[9] Frankly, any amount of interest is too much.

Wrong.

Soon, you are at a point where you need to drastically cut your monthly expenses JUST to start paying your credit cards down. But you have your mortgage, rent, utilities, food, insurance, phone, internet, etc. that MUST be paid no matter what. Meanwhile your credit card bills keep growing.

Welcome to America. This is how many families live - in a debt spiral. Unfortunately it will get worse and worse and you will feel the impending doom unless you take drastic measures to get out. The best thing is to never get in that situation to begin with. This madness MUST stop.

That's why Neighborhood Millionaires never buy anything they cannot afford to pay cash for.

If you cannot pay actual cash for a purchase, you cannot afford it[10]. There is no shame in this. In fact,

---

[10] Okay, there is one exception to this rule and that is a primary residence. We will talk about buying a home later.

there should be a great deal of pride. Refusing a purchase you can't afford is the uncommon common sense most people need!

A simple question to ask whenever you are considering debt for a purchase is this one: "Do I want this enough to spend my future freedom on it?" In reality, that's what you're doing.

But how do you ensure you spend less money than you make? How do you change your life and NEVER go back to the old ways?

It's not difficult at all. It takes discipline but it's not difficult. For starters, you need a budget. That's what we'll tackle next.

But before you turn the page, close your eyes and say out loud:

"I am becoming The Neighborhood Millionaire."

Chapter 6 - Four Steps to Setting a Budget That Works

A budget sounds like a nasty, horrible thing. In reality, it's the key to freedom. Just like traffic lights keep you from getting smashed by a truck on the highway, budgets keep you from getting killed financially.

Remember Dr. Paul from Chapter 4 who "only" needed another $30,000 to support his lifestyle? If he'd had a budget for each step of his career, this would have never been an issue. He could have added more and more luxuries to his budget the wealthier he became. Imagine how much lower his stress level would have been!

Instead, he put the luxuries first, fought off the guilt that came with them every step of the way, and still had to deal with the pain of being fake rich!

Creating and sticking to a household budget is absolutely imperative if you are going to be the Neighborhood Millionaire. As you will find out, it will be one of the most powerful, freeing, and life-changing moves you ever make. Generally speaking, most people who create a budget immediately feel like a tremendous weight has been lifted from their shoulders. It's likely you're making more money than you think… but it's all rushing out the door because you don't have a plan for it!

We'll create a simple sheet called a "zero-sum budget." That means every dollar you make has an assignment. Before spending a single dime, you put all your money in different categories.

Grab your notebook and let's get going.

Step 1:
The first step is writing down how much you make each month. If you don't know what you have, then how will you know what to budget? Write your

monthly income down at the top of your page. This is the actual dollar amount you[11] put in the checking account, and the absolute maximum you can spend. We will call this TOTAL MONTHLY TAKE HOME PAY (TOTALPAY).

Please be honest. Do not fudge it or exaggerate it as that will become a big problem for you later on.

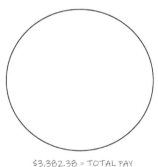

$3,382.38 = TOTAL PAY

---

[11] Or anyone else in your home.

Step 2:

Make a list of your mandatory expenses that you MUST pay every month to live. These include rent/mortgage payment, food and utilities. These are the items that if you do not pay, you will starve, freeze to death, or become homeless! Let's call these MUST-PAY-THESE-OR-I'M-HOMELESS (MUSTS) expenses!

Subtract the total of these MUSTS expenses from your TOTALPAY and now you have an idea how much you have available for other expenses.

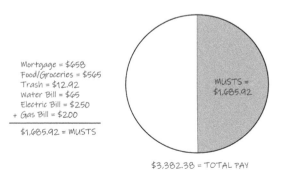

Mortgage = $658
Food/Groceries = $565
Trash = $12.92
Water Bill = $65
Electric Bill = $250
+ Gas Bill = $200
_____
$1,685.92 = MUSTS

MUSTS = $1,685.92

$3,382.38 = TOTAL PAY

Step 3:

Now make a note of your other important expenses (NEEDS). This includes phone bills, internet, car expenses, taxes, insurance, home repair and maintenance, clothing, and so on. DO NOT include optional items such as vacations, dining out, gym memberships, entertainment, etc. Subtract the NEEDS total from your TOTALPAY as well.

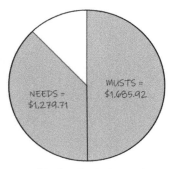

Student Loan = $300
Car Payment = $250
Car Insurance = $144.09
Car Registration = $75
Gasoline = $100
Internet = $105.62
Credit Card = $255
+ Dog Food/Meds = $50
——————————
$1,279.71 = NEEDS

MUSTS = $1,685.92

NEEDS = $1,279.71

$3,382.38 = TOTAL PAY

Step 4:

Next, list out all those nice things you like to buy from month-to-month (WANTS) These are the optional things that you can do without such as vacations, entertainment, gifts, dining out, cable, gym, manicures, HBO, Netflix, etc.

Go ahead and write down the total for these items as well. Once you have your WANTS, put that number to the side.

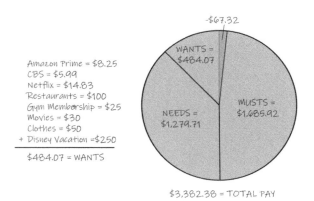

Amazon Prime = $8.25
CBS = $5.99
Netflix = $14.83
Restaurants = $100
Gym Membership = $25
Movies = $30
Clothes = $50
+ Disney Vacation =$250

$484.07 = WANTS

-$67.32

WANTS = $484.07

MUSTS = $1,685.92

NEEDS = $1,279.71

$3,382.38 = TOTAL PAY

If TOTALPAY minus MUSTS minus NEEDS minus WANTS is a positive number, congratulations! You are doing well and you still have some money to work with. If that total is a negative number (like in the example above), you are already spending more than you earn and something needs to be fixed right now.

Most likely, you have categorized a WANT as a MUST or NEED. Take a second look at your list now to see how critical those items are. After that, start chopping off WANTS until you reach a positive number at the end of your sheet.

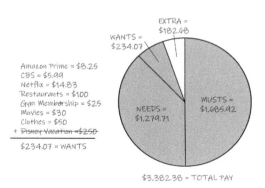

Be honest with yourself. If every single item on the list is critical, and you're still negative, you are either in total denial, or you're paying too much for a home, car, or clothing[12].

Once you've done the necessary work to get a positive number, you'll take whatever money is left to pay off debt, stock up a larger emergency fund, or invest. We'll discuss all of these options and the order you should do them) shortly. The important thing to remember is that not a single dollar is left unbudgeted. See the example below:

$3,382.38 = TOTAL PAY
$1,685.92 = MUSTS
$1,279.71 = NEEDS
$234.07 = WANTS
+ $182.68 = EXTRA (for debt or savings)
_____

$0

---

[12] We'll talk more about how to reduce these costs later in the book.

That's it! Once you have your budget in place, you are on the way to freedom.

Keep your budget on paper for the first three months like I showed you in the example above. Whenever you feel you are comfortable with it, though, I'd recommend transferring it to a digital tool like Mint.com.

There are tons of software programs and apps that can help you with your budgeting, but Mint is my favorite. It is extremely powerful but easy to use. Best of all it is totally free![13] You can find it on your computer's browser as well as in the app store for iPhones and Androids.

---

[13] If you don't use Mint, be aware that some apps appear to be "free," but once you begin using them they start to charge you for features. Don't spend money on a simple budgeting tool when you don't have to!

Never forget, without a budget you are going about this whole thing blindly. And driving blind is a good way to go off a cliff.

Now, before you turn the page, close your eyes and say out loud:

"I am becoming The Neighborhood Millionaire."

Chapter 7 - How to Use Your New Budget

The true power of a budget is that it makes choices for you. No more agonizing over whether or not you should spend. No more fighting with guilt over an impulsive purchase.

You only need to ask: does my budget allow me to buy this?

If the answer is yes, feel free to buy it.

If the answer is no, don't buy it.

Easy, right? The budget decides so you don't have to.

It does not matter how much or how little money you make. Multimillionaires need a budget as well as those who earn a modest income.

By the way, you've built a budget that is *dynamic*. That means every time you make more money, you must update your budget before you update your spending. If you have a budget for your income which is $75,000, and your boss doubles your salary to $150,000, then you need to re-work your budget so it finishes at $0 again[14]. Please note this does not mean you need to spend $75,000 more on random *stuff* to make the math work. I'll show you what I mean shortly, but first, let me tell you about my friend Anthony.

Anthony is a writer who does well for himself, and he is also very savvy with money. A while back, he and a woman hit it off on their first date, so the woman suggested they go to a special restaurant to celebrate their second date.

Since Anthony liked the woman, he agreed to a more expensive meal. Naturally, he adjusted his budget to include a certain amount for the evening.

---

[14] Also, you need to pat yourself on the back because that sort of raise is AWESOME.

Upon entering the restaurant, though, he discovered that this was not just a nice place, it was over-the-top expensive! Five courses. Expensive wine. Fine pairings. Anthony quickly calculated that with a little wine, tax and gratuity, the evening would cost him at least $500.

That was more than the budget allowed.

He very politely told his date that they would not be dining there that evening and asked her to pick another place. Can you guess what happened? His date went to the restroom and never again reappeared. Anthony made the right decision. Could Tony afford to drop $500 on a dinner? Sure. It likely would not have affected his overall financial plan. But it wasn't in the budget. He hadn't planned for it. As it turned out, he made the right call. Who would want to be with a person who crawls out the window after you suggest spending less on a meal?

This is the importance of a budget. You will be able to make decisions based on your plan and not on emotions! This is powerful. When you put your feelings in charge, you might make the right choice. When you put your budget in charge, you can't make the *wrong* choice.

Follow your budget. Live within your means. Make no excuses. Start now.

Before you turn the page, close your eyes and say out loud:

"I am becoming The Neighborhood Millionaire."

Chapter 8 - Why Many Millionaires Are Miserable

How would it feel to make a million dollars a year? I bet you would say it would feel awesome. I say it depends.

The person who makes a million dollars per year who *also* has expenses amounting to a million dollars (or more) is set up for disaster. Although that person has a lot of "things" and probably takes the nicest vacations, life is stressful. Very stressful.

In order for this person to keep up the million-dollar lifestyle, they MUST keep making that money month after month, year after year. There is no reprieve. I call this living in "Golden Handcuffs." Your friends, neighbors and relatives may envy you, but they have no idea how stressful your life may be!

That's why budgeting and living within your means matters so much.

The psychological and physical cost of making a million dollars a year is enormous if you don't control that money. If you have to work all the time, be away from the family, go through undue stress, do work you do not enjoy, and stay indoors grinding away, what's the point? Watching your bank account consistently fill all the way up only to fall all the way back down is a miserable experience.

Worse, suppose that million-dollar job suddenly dries up. Imagine there is a weird event that turns your town, a country, or even the world upside down. Suppose that secure business takes a turn for the worst? Most people believe it could never happen to them.

Well, at least before COVID they did.

The Coronavirus showed us just how fragile our economy is. Many friends who used to make a LOT of money in "secure" jobs suddenly made nothing. Dentists went out of business. Restaurants closed.

Travel froze. Vacations stopped. Thriving retail areas turned into sites of protests, riots and occupations.

Trust me, you are not immune. The Coronavirus wasn't the first event to shake up our world, and it won't be the last.

The idea of out-earning a budget is fool's gold. You can't do it. It's NOT really about making more and more money. It's about being smarter and smarter. It's about building up real financial security through living below your means.

> **The psychological and physical cost of making a million dollars a year is enormous if you don't control that money.**

A couple earning $80,000 a year, living on $60,000, and investing $20,000 every year has MUCH less stress and perhaps much more happiness than the couple earning $1,000,000 and spending all or most of it.

But of course you still want to become the Neighborhood Millionaire! Why? Because in addition to being wealthy, the Neighborhood Millionaire basically has no financial stress. We are regular people. We are not flashy and feel no desire to "keep up" with others.

In a few short chapters you have learned the three most important principles to joining the ranks of Neighborhood Millionaires:

- Setting clear goals to aim for
- Spending less money than you make
- Creating a budget every month

It's important to pause here because, once again, you must remember how important those three steps are. They are the key to becoming a Neighborhood Millionaire instead of yet another Fake Millionaire. I do not want you to only have wealth and a big fat income. I want you to have joy and a stress-free life. With these principles you can do just that.

If you have actually set goals, accepted the principle of living within your means, and created your first budget, you are already on your way to becoming wealthy.[15] I promise. As the old song goes, "we've only just begun!"

Now, before you turn the page, close your eyes and say out loud:

"I am becoming The Neighborhood Millionaire."

---

[15] And if you haven't GO BACK and reread Chapters 1-7 again.

Chapter 9 - Build a Roof Over Your Finances for Rainy Days

Now that you have your budget in place, let's address the steps for using that extra money.

Your very first goal is to save a preliminary emergency fund.

A credit card is not an emergency fund. Cash is. Cash reserves provide the first step to fearlessness when life throws messes your way. How much money do you have lying around in case an emergency arises? A scary statistic is that 69% of Americans have less than $1000 in savings. Are you one of them?

You're probably eager to use that budget for paying off debt, but the emergency fund must come first. This preliminary fund protects you from the little bumps of life, and it keeps you from running to a credit card which obviously leads to MORE debt, not less.

What does that look like in real life? Take another look at the budget from Chapter 6

```
   $3,382.38 = TOTAL PAY
   $1,685.92 = MUSTS
   $1,279.71 = NEEDS
   $234.07 = WANTS
 + $182.68 = EXTRA (for debt or savings)
─────────────────────────────────────────
   $0
```

As you can see, there is $182.68 left over in this example budget. All of that money goes directly into the preliminary emergency fund. That can be a scary step to take. But if you've done your budget correctly, there's no need to put that money anywhere else, right? That's exactly what the extra money is for.

This money will be used in case of emergencies only - true emergencies. An emergency by definition is an expense you didn't expect that must be paid right away. An emergency is not a craving to eat at a restaurant or stick your toes in the sand!

The emergency fund is ONLY for emergencies![16]

Think about it this way. When you're driving your car down the interstate, what's on the side of the road? A shoulder. Why is it there? To leave room for error. If you get distracted, if you swerve, if you make a mistake, the shoulder keeps you out of trouble. The emergency fund functions the same way. It's there to give you a little grace when life gets hard.

---

[16] Did I say that enough yet?

Your first goal is to save $1000. Keep it safe in a bank savings account where you can reach it at any time. Remember, if you've done this, you are in the top 30% of Americans! Once you hit that goal, give yourself a pat on the back. Put on your favorite song and dance around the kitchen.

Next, you'll keep piling up cash until you hit that $2000 number. Is it perfect? No. Will it cover literally every emergency? No. That's why it's a *preliminary* emergency fund.

You can start on your emergency fund right away. Once you do, you can move on to the next step - paying back that debt and reclaiming your freedom.

Now, before you turn the page, close your eyes and say out loud:

"I am becoming The Neighborhood Millionaire."

Chapter 10 - Prepare to Rid Yourself of Debt… Forever

There are many so-called "experts" out there that claim some debt is good and you should use other people's money to acquire what you want in life.

I disagree.

On my road to becoming a Neighborhood Millionaire, I have seen too many failures. Debt is a demon that will cripple your overall financial plan to fail. I can say that with complete confidence because I believed the "good debt" myth for way too long. After having done it both ways, I can assure you that rejecting debt of any kind is the shortest, most stress-free path to financial freedom.

One part of financial health is simple making the right choices. That's why we started these with your dreams, your goals, your lifestyle, and your budget. The other part is *avoiding* the wrong choices. Debt is the wrong choice. That's why it will be a curse word for the remainder of this book.

Do you have ANY debt other than your home? Be honest. Any credit cards? Student loans? Car loans? Medical bills? Phone payments? If your answer is no, congratulations to you. You are doing fantastic... better than most of the people in the country! Please skip to the next chapter only after agreeing that you will NEVER again take on any debt. Great job!

If you DO have debt, let's make a promise today that you will do everything in your power to get rid of it as soon as possible. Neighborhood Millionaires don't have debt.

Grab that notebook again and we will begin an exercise to help you ditch the debt for good.

On the next empty page of your notebook, list your smallest debt first. Do not worry about the interest rate on each debt, just take the smallest debt you have and write that down first. Next, list the second smallest. Then the third. Continue this process until you have listed every single one of your debts from smallest to largest. Hopefully, you won't use *too* many lines.

Once you do this, add up the total.

After you gasp, capture this feeling. It's awful, right? If you're like most Americans, you're likely looking at a number close to $90,000. That could be twice or three times your salary at this point. Many people avoid calculating their total debt simply to avoid the pain you're feeling right now. Hold on to this hot panic. You'll need every emotion you can whip up to really move the needle in your life.

PROMISE yourself RIGHT NOW that you will get this paid off and then never again go into debt. You wouldn't play with a stick of dynamite, and you don't need to play with debt either.

Removing the cancer of debt from your life will probably not be an easy task, no matter how much you have[17]. It depends on how much debt you have, your income, your expenses and your lifestyle. But the most important thing I can tell you is that you have to attack this with a vengeance, as if you HATE debt and will do whatever it takes to get it out of your life forever.

Since you've already got your preliminary emergency fund built, take every penny of extra money you have each month and put it toward the first item on your debt sheet.

Huge companies have spent millions of dollars making debt seem like it isn't urgent. It is urgent. Don't hesitate. Don't fall into bad habits. Don't put off this step simply because you have a few bucks in your bank account.

---

[17] One reason for this is that credit card companies will do EVERYTHING in their power to keep bleeding your bank account dry, including offers for double points, increased limits, and "exclusive" memberships. Avoid this garbage.

Once you pay off that first item in the list, you'll receive a raise. How? Because in addition to no longer paying absurd interest charges on a loan, you also no longer have a minimum payment! You've got *even more* extra money! Use it to throw at the next debt. The next debt paid off will result in *another* raise.

Forget begging bosses for a 2% merit increase. Paying off debt gives you control over your own money, starting immediately.

This process is what we call a virtuous cycle. The more you do it, the better it gets. Believe me when I say the first debt is the hardest to pay off. If you stick to the plan, each one gets easier. Bill after bill will tumble to the ground like dominos, all because you had the courage to take that first step.

Imagine what it would feel like to shake that $120 phone bill. Visualize the freedom that comes after that $198 credit card charge disappears. Dream of how much you could do once that $410 car payment is gone.

Powerful, right? You're on the path right now[18].

Now, before you turn the page, close your eyes and say out loud:

"I am becoming The Neighborhood Millionaire."

---

[18] The most common question I get asked at this point is "How can I pay off my debt when I can hardly afford to pay my monthly bills?" Don't worry, we'll talk about fast-tracking your way to earning more income, saving more, and paying off debt in the next section of this book.

Chapter 11 - Your Extended Emergency Fund

Once you are debt-free, it's time to move to the next step.

Now, don't panic here. All you did was flip a page, and now I'm talking about debt freedom! But depending on how much debt you have, the amount of time it will take you to pay it off will vary.It could be a month or two, but it could be years.

If you focus and attack the debt like nothing you have ever attacked in your life, your life will feel different. You will feel free. You will put your head on your pillow each and every night knowing that no matter what happens in the world, in the country, to the economy… that you have NO PAYMENTS.

What on Earth does a person do with no payments??

Later, you use it to invest and build your path to becoming the Neighborhood Millionaire.

Right now, though, we're going to use it to make your finances as bulletproof as possible. If you want to build a skyscraper of wealth, you need a rock-solid foundation.

In Chapter Nine, you built an emergency fund of $1000 to $2000. That was a good start, but it was a temporary fix. We needed to put out the debt fire.

Now that you are debt free, we need to increase your emergency fund to six months of your living expenses.

Let's say your monthly expenses are $5,000. This means your emergency fund will need to be at least six times that number - $30,000. Keep this money set aside as a pure emergency fund to be used ONLY in true emergencies. It should not be invested in the stock market or real estate. Just keep it in a bank savings account where it is not at risk and it can be accessed immediately if needed.

This emergency fund is there for you when "life happens." You may lose a job, get laid off temporarily, have a bad few months in your business, have a medical emergency... things definitely happen in life and they happen to everyone. You are not immune. None of us are. Trust me.

Once you have your full emergency fund set up, another load of stress will be taken away from you. Your mind will be so much more at peace.

These feel like small steps, but that's where any long journey starts. Besides, what's the point of starting if you have to start all over again?

You want to become the Neighborhood Millionaire? This is the way to do it. There are no shortcuts. You can do it, but you must take the steps in order.

Now, before you turn the page, close your eyes and say out loud:

"I am becoming The Neighborhood Millionaire."

Chapter 12 - Make More Money Doing What You Love

There are two sides to this money game. One is how much money you are making - your income. The other is how much you are spending - your expenses. Both have to be in check to your lifestyle. No matter how thorough your budget is, too little income is bad news. If you don't have cash to feed your family, keep a roof over your head, and run some heat and running water, you need to make more money.

It's as simple as that.

Once you have your mental foundation in place (goals, lifestyle, budget), a larger income means it is easier to achieve financial freedom. It will turn your walk toward your goals into a dead-out sprint.

So how do you make more money?

It's a stupid question to some but the answer, unless you are a trust fund baby or a scammer, is work.

Now you may cringe when you hear the word "work." Don't. What if I told you that you could earn more money AND be happier than ever while doing it? Work doesn't have to be a bad thing, especially if it's that lever that lifts you into Neighborhood Millionaire status.

Today, work is like a vacation to me. I absolutely *love* what I am doing. This is true today, as I'm sitting on my front porch, staring at the mountains in Salt Lake City with a cup of tea typing these words on my MacBook, but it was also true back when I started to transform my own financial future.

Although it is beyond the scope of this book to teach you how to get a better job or start a business, I've always found it helpful to read stories about how other people built wealth. I'll tell you mine now.

I started off my professional career as a dentist because my mom just pounded the idea into my head. Every day she would say "repeat after me - dentistry is a great profession!" If I did not repeat it, she got angry at me and would withhold my dessert.

Even though I knew NOTHING about what working as a dentist for the rest of my life would look like, I took the bait. I got accepted into dental school and turned in a mediocre performance at best... but I did graduate in the top 90% of my class!

I took a one-year general practice residency afterwards and a couple of awful associateships (working for other dentists). At some point, I had the crazy idea to open my own dental practice in beautiful Ellicott City, Maryland with Steve, a dental buddy of mine.

Starting a dental practice, or any type of business, is NEVER easy. There is a lot of work that goes into it as well as a lot of risk. I would say the first few years were tough, but we experienced some good growth.

After a fairly short amount of time Steve and I were earning very nice livings.

Life was good.

Or was it?

Most people looking in from the outside would say that Dr. Dave had it made. The problem was Dr. Dave looking in the mirror inside his dental office every day and sighed. Dentistry was not something that he wanted to do forever, and maybe he'd never wanted to do it at all.

So instead of "going with the program" that so many people do for their entire lives, I decided to take action. In addition to my dental office, I started exploring other opportunities. I set up some other "side businesses" and immersed myself in the marketing, writing, speaking and sales cultures. I experimented. I tried things. With every failure (and there were a lot), I learned a lesson.

One day, out of the clear blue sky, I ordered 500 business cards printed up that said "DMM Management Consultants." Even though I had absolutely NO IDEA what DMM Management Consultants did, it felt good to have these cards and it definitely got my creative juices flowing! I felt proud handing them out to everyone I would meet.

After about five years of trial and error, I found a hit. One of the businesses I set up happened to be with my brother Rich, who is also a dentist. We began by selling dental collection forms by direct mail out of Rich's home. Our "office" was a kitchen table, a pickup truck and a telephone answering machine. Seriously.

Every Monday evening after working at our own dental practices, we would meet up at the local post office box to collect the orders that had come in during that previous week. Some Mondays it would be stuffed so full that we literally had to stick a long ruler in the box to wedge the envelopes out.

And guess what the cool thing was? Every single envelope order had a big fat check inside of it! (This was still way before the internet, so everyone paid by check!)

Rich and I lived and breathed this stuff every single day. We were having a blast. We ultimately became very well known in the dental profession as "Key Opinion Leaders," speakers, consultants and much more.

After a few years of this "side business," I was able to sell my portion of my dental practice back to Steve as I simply did not want to practice dentistry any longer. I was having too much fun! More than thirty years later, the business that brother Rich and I started on the side, "The Madow Center" (www.madow.com) is still a thriving force in the dental profession.

It started with an idea.

It started with a refusal to give in to life.

It started with action.

I don't tell you all this to brag. I tell you this because I was clueless, I tried things anyway, and now I get to live the Neighborhood Millionaire lifestyle every single day.

What a gift!

If you are in a job or a business that you do not love or one that stresses you out, do not quit. At least, don't quit yet. Instead, build a side hustle. And since you must make money anyway, do it through what you love. After all, my brother and I found our big idea having the time of our lives. To say the internet opened up a world of opportunities is an understatement. Your possibilities are infinite!

In your search for the right business or job, PLEASE do not be like my friend Bobby. We all call him "Benzo Bobby" and I'll tell you why. You see, Bobby is a very successful businessman in his own right. Not only does he own companies that do business all over the world, he also owns a ton of real estate as well as other investments. He owns several homes that he and his wife alternate their time between. Benzo Bobby has enough money to do pretty much whatever he wants in life.

So what's the problem? You see, Bobby lives such a stressful life every single day that he needs to take Benzodiazepines (anti-anxiety medications such as Valium and Xanax) for breakfast, lunch and dinner. Being addicted to Benzos is basically the only way Bobby can exist and get through the day.

Everyone on the outside envies Benzo Bobby, but I would not trade places with him for all of the money in the world. I prefer to be the Neighborhood Millionaire, where I have just enough money, I do not need to flaunt it, and I am able to live my life to the absolute fullest.

So to recap, there are many manuals for success, but the best advice I can give you is this:

Think. Dream. Try. Learn. Figure it out. Read your goals from Chapter Two as often as you can. I even give you permission to print up business cards for your dream job/business. Work your job or your business because you are passionate about it, and not solely to make "tons of money!"

If you don't stand up for yourself, who will?

Now, before you turn the page, close your eyes and say out loud:

"I am becoming The Neighborhood Millionaire."

Chapter 13 - Pep Talk

Okay. We have accomplished a lot so far, so let's do a quick recap. As of right now, you have:

- Set goals to guide you forward
- Accepted living within your means
- Built a budget for your household
- Socked away a starter emergency fund
- Kicked your crappy debt to the curb
- Filled the emergency fund to the max
- Started daydreaming of new ways to make more money

Congratulations. You are doing great.

I do realize that if you are reading this book for the first time, you have likely not actually completed all of the above. But take a moment to feel how your mind is working in overdrive now. Can you see your new life? Can you envision the difference? Can you feel the freedom? Your life is changing *right now*.

Please do me a favor, though. Stay 100% committed to getting this done. Reading the plan is pretty easy. *Living* the plan takes tremendous commitment. But the way I see it, there is no other choice. If you reject responsibility (the way so many people do in this country), you will always be broke and your retirement will be bleak. You don't want that. I don't want that for you.

I want to be clear, though: what we've talked about this far are **The First Steps**. Setting a household budget and spending less money than you make are principles that you will keep in place no matter how much money you make in the future, even when you are debt free. Don't compromise on these principles. It's far too easy to go back into debt if you do.

We've got two more sections to go:

The Fast Track, which contains rules and lessons that help you complete the first steps as fast as possible.

The Future, which helps you build an unbreakable fortress around your finances[19].

Ready to move forward? Let's go.

Before you turn the page, close your eyes and say out loud:

"I am becoming The Neighborhood Millionaire."

---

[19] It will be tempting to skip here, especially if you're still scraping by paycheck to paycheck. However, just like a house, you have to build the ground floor first.

The Fast Track

Chapter 14 - Playing Defense

Most of America is broke.

This is partly because they don't do the right things and partly because **they keep doing the wrong things**.

There is SO MUCH misinformation out there about building wealth, it's scary! Everyone has their story, a tip on how to get rich, what to do, what not to do, etc. Unfortunately most are WRONG and will get you into trouble. That's why this section is dedicated to some general principles to guide you through common pitfalls of wealth building.

My job as your Neighborhood Millionaire coach is to get you there soon, not seventy years from now! That's why this section is dedicated to accelerating your journey to financial freedom. The more lessons you take to heart, the faster you can go.

Remember, once you become a Neighborhood Millionaire, you can live your life very differently. For now, be patient and keep working the system.

Let's dive in.

Before you turn the page, close your eyes and say out loud:

"I am becoming The Neighborhood Millionaire."

Chapter 15 - The Most Common Cause of Financial Destruction: Family Disagreements

Why do people get divorced? Nobody walks down the aisle, looking at the love of their life and thinks: "I can't wait to scream at this person over who gets the good plates." Weddings are about the promise of forever.

Yet, many relationships end in a bitter separation. Money disagreements are one of the leading causes for these unhappy endings.

Let's say you are reading this book now and you are 100% on board with becoming the Neighborhood Millionaire. Here's the problem: your partner hasn't read a single page.[20] Whenever you come in spouting crazy dreams about getting rich, it's likely you'll get nothing but an eye roll in return. If you and your

---

[20] Unless you are reading together. In that case - you ROCK!

spouse aren't on the same page about all of this, you WILL have problems. I guarantee it.[21]

On some level I lucked out with my wife. She and I are totally on the same page when it comes to money and life. We both embrace the Neighborhood Millionaire mindset. Our cars, our home, our clothes… everything about us says that we are just "regular people." We are. We love to have fun, travel, and do all of the outdoor activities that everyone else does here in Utah.

The only real difference between us and many people is that we are millionaires. We can pretty much do anything we want, go on any trip we like, and live in any city, state or country we wish. Although sometimes we go on crazy adventures, we are grounded and never take advantage of what we have worked so hard to achieve.

_____

[21] If you are single and never plan to have a partner of any type, you should still read this chapter. Life has a funny way of wrecking plans.

We are Neighborhood Millionaires in the flesh.

Imagine what would happen to our marriage if we did not have the same beliefs and outlooks on money. If Yoko was a frugal saver, and I was a flashy spender, that would be a formula for disaster. I do not have to tell you how that could end up.

Instead, we are on the same page. Not only that, but we *stay* on the same page. Just because two people agree on certain principles early in life doesn't mean it will stay that way. I told you earlier in the book that we have annual meetings about our financial picture so we each know exactly where we are. Obviously we stay in touch all year long about this but our New Year's meeting is our most comprehensive. Again, none of these meetings are fancy. Most often, we meet in a quiet restaurant with our laptops and our notebooks full of goals. From month to month, we chat across the kitchen table.

So let me ask you, are you and your spouse or life partner on the same financial page? For that matter, do you actually have the same life goals? Be honest and answer those questions. You do not have to share with me, but you need to know this.

> **If you and your spouse aren't on the same page about all of this, you WILL have problems.**

The sooner you can have a serious discussion with your partner, the better. Talking solves problems. Not talking makes problems worse. It can feel awkward to do this, especially if you don't talk about money much now. However, it's much better to have an awkward conversation about building your wealth than to have the awkward one about how to split it in half.

As we've seen in society, the smallest pebble of a problem in a relationship can grow to become an impossible boulder. Communicate your honest thoughts with your spouse, starting now.

It's not enough for you and your partner alone to be on the same page about spending money on each other. You also have to be in agreement on how to spend it on your children. Otherwise, you'll end up like a reader of mine named Liz.

Liz is a single retired nurse who dedicated her life to caring for others. Although this is an admirable enough choice regardless of the paycheck, she made a very nice living throughout her working life.

Sadly, she has very little to show for it all right now. The reason? Her adult children.

Liz could never manage to say "no" to her kids whenever they asked for help. She'd "lend" them a few hundred bucks here and there whenever they asked. She bought them cars because she wanted them to have a leg up. In the end, Liz ended up giving everything away. That sounds noble, but now her retirement fund is puny. She is rightly worried about her future.

Worse, her children won't be able to save her. How could they? They've always had a financial safety net named "Mom." What started as goodwill is now a scary situation. It's very possible that both Liz and her kids could be in big trouble. Liz would change her mind if she could go back in time.

If you have family members who need help, please be very careful. Your financial health is more important than the car that little Johnny "needs" to have. Understand that when it comes to financial health, you must secure yourself first. There are so many "Liz's" out there who give and give and give to family members only to end up with nothing[22]. Honestly, the horror of that keeps me awake some nights.

---

[22] By the way, it is not wrong to give. We will be discussing that very soon.

Please make sure you and your family members understand that there are boundaries, and you have to stick to them. Oftentimes the word "no" is the most powerful word in the English language.

Before you turn the page, close your eyes and say out loud:

"I am becoming The Neighborhood Millionaire."

Chapter 16 - The Credit Card Dilemma

The most common Neighborhood Millionaire killer is something you likely have in your wallet or purse right at this very moment. A credit card!

Now unlike a very popular financial guy on the radio, I am not totally against credit cards. I use them. But I do use them very carefully, which means:

I buy only what I can afford.
I pay my credit card off as soon as the bill comes.
Every single month.
No exceptions.
Never late.

The credit card is a good tool, especially these days when touchless payment options are available such as Apple Pay, Google Pay, etc. Also, many businesses simply refuse to take a debit card for payment, like rental car establishments and several phone, cable, satellite and internet providers. Debit cards have some limitations. Plastic without a Visa or MasterCard logo might be frowned upon when you travel. While debit cards can be rejected once you leave your town, credit cards can be accepted virtually anywhere in the world. That is another reason I carry a credit card - the flexibility.

However, problems start when you violate the careful bullet points listed above. If you don't follow those guidelines, the bill that comes at the end of each month will make you want to jump off a cliff. Credit cards get a LOT of people into a LOT of trouble.

If in doubt, use a debit card. It's safer. Why? Because when you use a debit card, you are essentially using your own cash. The money is immediately taken out of your bank account. That means no looming charges to worry about at the end of the month! When you use a debit card it affects you psychologically almost like cash. You think a little harder before making the purchases. Thinking is a good thing, by the way.

The best way to avoid the pains that come with credit card debt is to avoid it entirely in the first place. I have seen so many people's lives literally ruined from credit card debt that just becomes extremely difficult to pay off. Do not get started. Remember, if you're rolling along the path I outlined in the first section, you may still be paying off credit card debt. That's fine… but don't pick up any more! Always remember "the borrower is slave to the lender!"

Before you turn the page, close your eyes and say out loud:

"I am becoming The Neighborhood Millionaire."

Chapter 17 - How NOT to Buy a Car (Part 1)

"I need a new car. How much should I spend?"

Sure you do! Everyone "needs" a new car!

Not.

All kidding aside, it is important to consider the best way (and the worst way) to purchase a vehicle. Even though most Americans need a car, many spend much more than necessary and wind up paying crazy interest rates on top of that. That's why cars are one of the greatest barriers to wealth. We buy more than we can afford. It's not uncommon these days to go into a dealership and come out sporting a nice $30,000 - $40,000 car, SUV or truck.

Remember my neighbor Chris that I spoke about earlier in the book? He is leasing a $40,000 SUV with a $55,000 income and credit card debt. Sadly, Chris is "normal" when it comes to Americans buying and leasing cars.

Now I am not "anti-automobile" in any way. I have cars. I'm not mad at Chris for getting a car. I just hate *what* he bought and *how* he bought it.

If you are not yet a Neighborhood Millionaire you should be extremely careful regarding what type of car or cars you are driving. I know this from experience.

I have made all of the typical mistakes that everyone makes with cars. In my younger days when I was just beginning to accumulate wealth, I thought it would be appropriate to be driving nice new foreign cars all the time. My first wife and I would go to the dealerships and leave with Volvo's, Saabs… you name it. They always looked shiny and brand new in our driveway. I am sure the neighbors were impressed.

We generally took out loans for these cars. How else could we buy them?

The height of my stupidity can be highlighted with a single vehicle - a Land Rover Discovery.

After we signed all of the lease papers for this luxury vehicle, Bobby, the owner of the dealership was so kind to us. He actually asked the manager to make sure we had a full tank of gas before we drove away from the dealership with our brand new vehicle. Wow! A full tank of gas! Can you imagine?! Never mind that the car that was ready to depreciate 20% as soon as we drove off the lot. Never mind that Bobby made an enormous commission off of the sale. I had a WHOLE tank of gas!

The story gets worse.

When the lease ended, we decided to buy the vehicle. So what did we do? We financed it for the full amount! That means that I not only paid to decrease the value of the car, I then bought it for full market value! We basically paid *twice* for the same set of wheels.

It gets even worse than that.

When my first wife and I divorced, I had to buy her out. Guess what was included in that settlement? Yep. The Land Rover. Do you know what that means? That means I essentially paid for that damn vehicle ***THREE TIMES!!!***

It doesn't get much stupider.

Cars are one of the greatest barriers to wealth.

Look around at your neighbors' cars. This may come as a surprise, but I am betting the ones who drive the fanciest eye-catching cars are the most broke. I have found this to be generally true over the years. There is something about shiny chrome on a bumper that makes people crazy.

If you think that buying anything with a motor is a path to wealth, I want to give you a wake-up call right now. All things with motors GO DOWN in value. In other words, they don't help you to become the Neighborhood Millionaire in any way. They are simply transportation. Since transportation is a necessity for most of us, I am going to share the smartest way to buy cars while staying on the path to wealth.

First of all, if you are in debt of any kind[23], find the cheapest car that works and pay cash. DO NOT take out another loan. Please! Pick out an ugly, reliable car that gets you where you need to go. Why? Because you are in debt and you CANNOT afford to buy a nice car right at this moment.

---

[23] (other than your primary residence)

Most people think of cars as a long-term decision. They aren't. Remember, you are working your plan to become the Neighborhood Millionaire. Does it really matter if you drive a heap of junk for a few months? Or even a year or two?

Secondly, if you need to buy a car and have zero debt, you still need to pay cash. Yep. That's right. Even if you *can* take out a loan for a car, don't. Refuse a loan and absolutely DO NOT LEASE. Leasing is the most expensive way to purchase a car. Buy something reasonable that you can afford to pay cash for. My ideal car is one that is a few years old, has a little mileage on it, but is in very nice condition. You can find these either locally or online.

The truth is there is simply no reason to buy new expensive vehicles. I am a multimillionaire and I drive a Volvo with 150,000 miles on it. And I love it! My wife has a ten-year-old Jeep that she keeps in perfect condition. We could walk into any dealership and buy any car we would want with cash. But why would we?

If you are a math nerd like I am, a good rule of thumb to follow is this: the total value of your cars (or anything with engines such as boats and RVs) should not equal more than one half of your annual income. For example, a family with a household income of $80,000 per year should own cars that are valued at less than $40,000.[24]

This is a tough one to get over. In this country we have such a love for nice shiny cars and trucks. As I said, I used to be the same way. But if you can suck it up and simply drive a "regular" car, I promise you that you will become the Neighborhood Millionaire much quicker.

Once you become a Neighborhood Millionaire, you can buy whatever car you want.

---

[24] Ideally MUCH less. But if you're paying cash for everything, feel free to indulge yourself.

You probably won't bother, but just knowing that you can is a good feeling.

Before you turn the page, close your eyes and say out loud:

"I am becoming The Neighborhood Millionaire."

Chapter 18 - How NOT to Buy a Car (Part 2)

You may be wondering why Dr. Dave, a Neighborhood Millionaire, drives a car that is fifteen years old with 150,000 miles on it. The answer is... because that money is better spent elsewhere.

Let's look at the math on this. My Volvo has been paid off for fifteen years. If I was like most Americans, I'd be spending $450 per month on a car payment on a six year loan. Over the six years, that's $32,000 I will never see a return on. This is likely for a car you supposedly bought for $25,000, but the interest dives deeper and deeper into your pockets!

If I invest that same money ($450 per month) into a decent mutual fund (returning 8%), that $25,000 car turns into $41,000 at the end of the six years![25]

---

[25] Fear not. We'll talk about exactly how to invest in a few chapters.

Which would you rather have? A beat up car that *might* be worth $6,000 once it's paid off? Or $41,000 dollars that continues to make more money every year?

I thought so too.

This same mindset is useful whenever you go to purchase a car. The $25,000 to $60,000 that you would use to buy something new can instead be invested in mutual funds making money *for* you as opposed to taking money *from* you. I call this a "win-win."

The day will come when I will definitely need to replace my beloved Volvo. What will I buy? I am not sure what make of vehicle exactly, but I can tell you this. It won't be new. It will likely be a two to three-year old car with low mileage that someone took really good care of. Oh, and I will pay cash of course! That way I don't get trapped in the debt spiral, and I don't spend sleepless nights watching the interest pile up.[26] Are you starting to get an idea what it feels like to be the Neighborhood Millionaire? I certainly hope so!

Before we leave this chapter, I would like to share a story about my friend Gary. I have known Gary most of my life. He's a great guy. He loves cars. For as long as I can remember, Gary has owned two cars at the same time even though he is a single guy.

Gary does not just play with "regular" cars. Gary loves high-end autos such as BMWs, Mercedes, Porches, Range Rovers, Infinitis, and Teslas! One day not so long ago I sat down and did a little "mental math" in my notebook about Gary. These aren't exact numbers, but I'm guessing they are pretty darn close.

Let's make an educated guess about Gary's financial situation. We'll look over a ten year period. Gary normally keeps a given car for a maximum of three

---

[26] Well… I'll still be watching interest pile up. But it will be interest going back into my pocket.

years, so we will use three years as his average time with a car.

Over any given ten-year period, Gary has purchased about seven cars. Now remember, he drives expensive cars, which means we can safely assign an average purchase price of $40,000 per car. I am being VERY conservative here because I know several of his cars have been in the $60,000 - $70,000 range.

That's roughly $280,000 of car purchases over the ten years. Let's be fair. I am sure that when he goes to sell one or trade one in, he gets some money for it.[27] Since cars depreciate the most in the first three years, I'll take $80,000 off the top for sales and trade-ins. This is again a conservative estimate, but it makes for easier math. We can estimate that Gary spent a net of $200,000 on cars in a ten-year period. Looking at my calculator, if Gary would have put that same $200,000 into mutual funds returning an

---

[27] Not a lot. Remember, dealerships wouldn't offer trade-ins if it didn't benefit them.

average of 8%, twenty years later he would have had a cool $431,785 in his investment account[28]. This is just *one* ten-year period of his life.

But Gary loves cars. So he puts his money there. I am not in any way shaming my friend Gary. He's a really nice guy. And did I tell you he loves cars?

We all get to choose how we live our lives. Gary chose cars over becoming a Neighborhood Millionaire. He makes a very handsome living, but because of his choices and his lifestyle, he will likely HAVE to work well into his late sixties and more likely into his seventies before he can afford to retire. He, like so many others, will be trapped in golden handcuffs.

Imagine if you could do any job, anywhere, at any time without having to slave over a desk to keep

---

[28] Feel free to use the math from this example for ANYTHING you plan on buying. Before you decide to buy, figure out what that money would be worth in the future if you invested it instead.

food on the table and wheels in the driveway. Imagine you shake off the need to impress other people because you know the ultimate goal of life is FREEDOM.

That's what we're after, and that's why we're being so careful with cars.

Before you turn the page, close your eyes and say out loud:

"I am becoming The Neighborhood Millionaire."

Chapter 19 - To Stay on Track, Stay at Home More Often

In my experience, those who cut deeply and quickly are much happier than those who try to make little sacrifices that don't *really* move the needle. My challenge is - it's hard to convince people to cut expenses aggressively.

I sound like a grouch. That isn't my goal. My goal is to show you that a few hard choices now can give you the easiest possible life down the road.

One simple, deep sacrifice you can make is to simply stay at home more often. Stay at home instead of going out to eat, and stay at home instead of going on vacation. Few other choices have as much of an impact on the average person's budget than these two.

Remember, you don't have to stay at home *forever*, and you don't have to stay out of restaurants *forever* - just for a little while. When you fully commit to becoming the Neighborhood Millionaire, your whole life will align around getting you there as quickly as possible. What good is wealth if you're reaching the end of your time on this planet when you get there?

Most Americans spend way too much on food. That's great news! Why? Because it means there is plenty of room for you to save. The truth is, if you are struggling with bills and drowning in debt, you have no business eating in restaurants anyway. Imagine how much you could save if you trimmed out restaurants, prepared meals to-go, takeout coffee shops and Grubhub.

Cutting out expensive meals can be difficult because today we don't just eat to survive. We eat to socialize, to meet new people, to impress a first date, or simply to get a change of scenery. But the question is: would you rather have a few nice meals now, or enjoy the comfortable life of being the Neighborhood Millionaire in a few short years?[29]

The same question applies to that next vacation you are looking forward to. Is a short trip full of expenses and overpriced knick knack souvenirs really worth the cost of your long-term financial health?

Vacations are a big source of accidental spending. The money doesn't stop when you book the hotel. The travel costs money. The meals cost money. The entertainment costs money. A $500 vacation can easily skyrocket to $2,500 or more. It's too easy to move into "vacation mode," where you aren't as cautious with your budget as you may be at home.

If you are still in the process of paying off debt, don't go on any vacations at the moment. If you are

---

[29] Frankly, sticking to the grocery store (so long as you don't buy lobster and steak each week) will probably keep you healthier anyway. There aren't many choices in life that can leave you richer and fitter!

debt-free, but not a millionaire, I still suggest going on the cheapest vacations possible. Make a reservation at a campground somewhere, throw a tent in the car, pack some food, drive there, and have a really great time. My wife and I still prefer that type of vacation today!

So many of us feel that we work hard and we "deserve" that wonderful vacation with our families. After all, we work hard, right? So you book those same expensive spots that everyone else gets in Ocean City or Vail. Maybe you take two trips a year. Maybe three. Suddenly, you are looking at the bank account wondering where all your money went!

Look, there is nothing inherently wrong with taking vacations, but when it comes to wealth-building, everything must be done in the proper order. Neighborhood Millionaires must be patient and put the work into achieving that status. Once you become one, you can basically do whatever you want. If you have the discipline now to live like people won't, then later you can do what other people can't.

Trust me, it's worth the wait!

Remember, if this was simple, everyone would be the Neighborhood Millionaire, right? It takes the knowledge and then perseverance! You can do this. You WILL do this.

Before you turn the page, close your eyes and say out loud:

"I am becoming The Neighborhood Millionaire."

Chapter 20 - College Loans Are Wealth Killers

With university costs skyrocketing in recent years, and American students in TRILLIONS of dollars of student loan debt, more families get put in the poorhouse each year in the name of education.

Let me start with the obvious. Education is good. It is one of the best investments we can make in ourselves. I went to both undergraduate college and dental school. I was fortunate enough to have my parents pay for everything.[30] However, college education is still a purchase. You are *buying* something. Whenever you buy something, you're looking for the best deal.

Just like Neighborhood Millionaires would never borrow money to put into the stock market because

---

[30] Thanks Mom and Dad!

it will "definitely" go up, we do not borrow money for college either.

Student loans might be the most destructive, life altering loans that you could EVER get your hands on. A student loan is almost never dismissible. That means even if you declare bankruptcy at some point, the student loan will have to be paid. They will come after you for the rest of your life to get that money.

Can you imagine how much stress you will have if you graduate owing $50,000? How about $100,000? I know people that have loans from professional or graduate schools to the tune of $250,000 and more. Think of how much you will have to earn to even begin paying those off! It is ludicrous.

So how does a future Neighborhood Millionaire who has little money pay for college? The key is to pursue *education* and not a degree.

First, and most importantly: **Find a school that fits your budget**. My parents were smart enough to restrict me only to schools they could afford. There is no real advantage to going to one of those exclusive, expensive schools if you cannot pay the bill for it. I have been a business owner for well over thirty years. I have hired hundreds of people in that time frame. Can you guess how many times the decision to hire someone was based on where they attended college or grad school?

NEVER.

I hired the people who would be best for my business. Where they went to school never entered the equation.

> **Student loans might be the most destructive loans that you could EVER get your hands on.**

Second, **pay for college as you go**: There is no shame in attending a local community college for your first couple of years and working a job at the same time to pay for your education. When I was in school, this was a pretty common choice. These days, it seems more important for kids to have the "experience" of college. In other words - partying at night, cutting classes, playing beer pong, and smoking weed.

Instead, why not find a job that can supply you with the income you need to "cash flow" your college education! It's called work! How is that for a novel idea?

Working yourself through school and living like a poor student is certainly one way to do it. For some, the military is also an option. Some programs offer full or most of tuition in exchange for time in the service. If you've been considering the armed forces anyway, this type of arrangement could be a fantastic experience which in itself could open up other career opportunities.

Third, **look for as many scholarships as possible**. Depending on your social demographics, your economic status, or your academics, you could qualify for various scholarships and grant programs. Most universities have funds set aside specifically for scholarships. If they don't use the funds, that money goes away. What does that mean? It means they *want* to spend scholarship money! Why shouldn't you get some?

It's easier than ever to find scholarship opportunities. Spend two hours alone with Professor Google, and I'm willing to bet you'll find more than enough opportunities to apply for.

The bottom line is this: **creativity beats debt**. Remember, no one owes you anything. Even if you do feel like you "deserve" a certain amount of education, you and I both know that you DON'T deserve to spend your whole life paying off non-bankruptable debt! Never, and I repeat: NEVER, take out a loan for your education.

Before you turn the page, close your eyes and say out loud:

"I am becoming The Neighborhood Millionaire."

Chapter 21: The Relief of Renting

I no longer own a home. That means I am a millionaire with no real estate. Some people will tell you this is impossible. I'm living proof that it isn't.

I owned homes for decades. Some of them were really nice homes! We really enjoyed the living. It was great coming home after work to a place that was *mine*. And the renters... well, I felt sorry for them. They were just throwing their money away every month with nothing to show for it!

At least that's what I thought.

A couple of years ago my wife Yoko and I decided we wanted a change in our lives. I had lived in Maryland all of my life and quite honestly I was getting a bit tired and bored of the east coast. We both LOVE the mountains and decided to move out west. We settled on Salt Lake City, Utah because it has something for everyone.

Before we moved here, we decided that we just had too much *stuff*. And take it from me, stuff turns to clutter which was not adding peace to our lives. Because a huge price comes both financially and mentally from owning a lot of *stuff*!

So we decided to simply sell or donate almost everything we owned before embarking on our new lives in Utah. I placed announcements and ads in local Facebook groups. Before we knew it we were down to owning only enough possessions that would fit in a small U-Haul pod that would ultimately be shipped out to Utah for when we got there. Plus, we felt good that so much of our stuff could find new owners.

We were so thrilled with the freedom that came from owning less that we went all the way. If we didn't want to own things, why would we own a home? That was the biggest change that came out of our lifestyle change. We did not buy a house in Salt Lake. We decided to rent!

This is probably the first time in my life since I graduated from dental school that I have not owned the house that I live in.

Renting has given us a ton of flexibility in our lives. All I do is write a rent check on the first of every month, and that gives me the freedom that we have worked SO HARD for my entire life. If something breaks down, I text the landlord and she normally takes care of the repair within hours. Zero stress for us. And I don't have to open up my checkbook. Since it's her property, she pays!

If Yoko and I decide that we want to relocate, it's simply a matter of informing the landlord and hitting the road. No real estate agent, no making repairs, no negotiating a price, no paying high commissions, and no risk of a deal falling through. None of that. We can just pick up and move to the beach if we choose with almost no expense!

Another great thing about renting is that we can't really make a mistake. If we rent a place that turns out to not fit us, we simply move as soon as the lease is up you move! Or if it's THAT bad, there are always ways of negotiating yourself out of a lease.

When I was a homeowner, I got a huge bill for property taxes every single summer. I had to write a check for thousands of dollars to the state of Maryland each year, and it certainly messed with my cash flow! Then there is insurance. When you own a home, you need thorough coverage which can get pricey quick. As a renter, I only need to purchase renters' insurance which is dirt cheap!

No repair costs. No property taxes. No long-term commitments. Dirt cheap insurance. We are LOVING this life!

Now, I know what you're thinking. "Dr. Dave, you big dummy. Don't you know that a home is a person's biggest asset? You're forgetting all about appreciation and throwing your money down the drain!"

This sounds good in theory. In reality, it's NEVER that simple. In fact, I've never experienced a big boom of appreciation in any of my homes. Several actually went *down* a bit in value by the time I sold. Being a homeowner for decades had nothing to do with me becoming the Neighborhood Millionaire. I could even speculate that I *lost* money in home ownership once all of the expenses were added up and taken into consideration.

Since I no longer own a home, I have a LOT of capital freed up to invest in the market. And even in average years, my investments in mutual funds will outperform the appreciation I would get from the money in a home. The reason a house is many people's biggest asset is simply because they don't *know* about any other ones!

The bottom line is that renting isn't just for college kids.

Now I want to reiterate: owning a home is not necessarily bad. In fact it could be quite good. The point is that instead of blindly buying a home because that's what "normal people" do, you should look at your notebook of goals, do your homework, do your math, figure out what you want your life to look like, and *then* make the decision.

I mentioned earlier that expensive cars are one of the big ways people ruin their financial life. Another common way is buying or renting a home beyond their means.[31] I am referring to your personal residence - the place where you live!

Here's a simple number to live by when moving into a home: 25%.

Your payment, whether it is a rent payment or a mortgage payment should be 25% or less of your total take home pay. If you violate this rule, it will be very difficult to become the Neighborhood Millionaire. If your total take-home pay is $8,000 per month, what is the most you can spend on rent or

---

[31] And we Neighborhood Millionaires live *within* our means... remember??

on a mortgage payment? If you said $2,000, you are correct. And of course it's always better to be well under that number.

Again, I'm not against buying a house or having a mortgage payment as long as you follow a few simple rules.

My first rule is that you MUST be able to make a down payment of at least 20%.

This will prevent you from paying PMI (private mortgage insurance) which is incredibly expensive and usually demonstrates that you cannot afford the house you are buying.

The second rule is that you take out a fixed rate mortgage with a term that is no longer than fifteen years.

Of course, your monthly payment must be equal to or less than 25% of your take home pay as stated above. By the way, the Neighborhood Millionaire will do whatever it takes to pay off their homes earlier than the fifteen-year term. They will "scratch and claw" and work extra jobs to get it done! We do not like debt of any kind! The goal here is to be completely debt-free.

Please, I never want to hear you say anything like "but I deserve a larger, more expensive home." That is simply not true. Numbers do not lie. You may feel that you "deserve" a more expensive home or a nicer car, but please remember… you are following certain rules now that will allow you to become the Neighborhood Millionaire later! Please do not waiver!

Before you turn the page, close your eyes and say out loud:

"I am becoming The Neighborhood Millionaire."

Chapter 22 - Three Common Pitfalls to Avoid

The theme of this chapter is "stay away." Imagine me saying it louder each time I write it.

First off, stay away from Multi-Level Marketing companies (MLMs).

MLMs are the biggest schemes created over the last many decades. To make matters worse, they are adapting well to the times. MLMs look better now than ever even though they are performing worse than ever. One reason these companies stay in business is because a miniscule percentage of people that get involved in MLMs actually do make a big chunk of money.

Most don't. Over 99% fall flat on their faces, and actually end up *losing* a ton of their own money. This is not my opinion. That scary statistic comes directly from the Federal Trade Commission website.

I am a capitalist and fan of hard work. But if you want to be a business owner, why not start a little business of your own? You would have a much better chance of starting a YouTube channel, Instagram page, or WordPress blog than you would with an MLM. Plus, you don't have to share the profits with anyone! Run toward these and stay away from MLMs.

Even the big name MLM companies that you have heard of can wreck your wallet. Stay far away. I will make some enemies by saying this, but I am not here to please anyone except YOU. You deserve the truth.

Speaking of the truth, let's step into another piece of it.

A timeshare is one of the biggest rip-offs known to man. STAY AWAY.[32]

---

[32] Told you I would get louder.

Now, you probably know timeshares are a bad deal, but you may end up with one anyway. Here's generally how people get sucked into them: You go to a presentation because you are offered some really nice gift. You say to yourself and to your partner, "Let's go. Let's do it. We will definitely say NO to any sales pitch and we will come away with this wonderful gift!"

Sounds easy enough, right? The problem is, the second you walk in the door, you will experience the highest pressure, most professional sales pitch ever. Even the most rational people can easily fall prey to these highly trained salesmen. By the end of the meeting, you'll be happy to hand over your payment. You sign your life away and not only do you get a rotten vacation deal, but you need to pay fees every month for the rest of your life.

Do not ever get involved on any level. Don't go to the meeting. Don't take the gift. Don't bite the bait. Ever.

There are thousands of "proud" timeshare owners that are trying to get out of them as we speak right now? It is virtually impossible. Don't believe me? Go online (start with eBay) and check out how many owners are trying to sell their timeshares for ONE DOLLAR. They cannot even give these things away.

Some companies claim they can get you out of a timeshare, but even these companies charge an enormous amount of money up front because these owners are so desperate to get out, they'll do anything.

Please never be even tempted to get involved with a timeshare. It can ruin your life.

Finally, STAY AWAY from ever co-signing a loan for someone else. I know you want to be kind. When your son, daughter, family member, friend, or co-worker ask you very nicely if you will co-sign that loan they are trying to get, you first say to yourself "What harm could come from just co-signing?"

I will answer your question with two words A LOT.

Once you cosign for a loan, it becomes YOUR loan. Think about it this way. The bank is not willing to give this person a loan because they feel it's too risky. So if a bank is not willing to give this friend or family member a loan, why in the heck would you ever consider for one split second to co-sign?[33]

Co-signing a loan can not only destroy your quest to become the Neighborhood Millionaire, it will very likely destroy your relationship with that person once they default and you are left holding the bag.

Please do not do it. Once you have actually reached all of your financial goals, if you feel generous, you can gift someone some money (meaning cash) to help them out. But I repeat, never cosign a loan! STAY AWAY.

---

[33] Think about how much time and money goes into a bank assessing risk. That's all they do. How could you possibly know better?

When you are the Neighborhood Millionaire, you can absorb the consequences of crazy or risky decisions. But, especially in the beginning of your wealth-building journey, it's much better to be smart than to be crazy.

Before you turn the page, close your eyes and say out loud:

"I am becoming The Neighborhood Millionaire."

Chapter 23 - Perseverance and Sacrifice

If you have read this far you certainly are serious about becoming the Neighborhood Millionaire. Good for you. Take a moment to pause once more, pull out your notebook, and begin to dream once again.

Jot down a few more thoughts about what it would feel like to be financially free. Describe the scene. Write a scenario. Spare no detail.

You will find that once you become a millionaire the way I teach, your life will totally change. You will *never again* be stressed about money. You will *never again* owe a dollar to anyone! You will *never again* have payments that eat through your wallet and your savings! Everything you own will be yours, and it will continue to grow into more!

But remember - becoming the Neighborhood Millionaire takes work. A lot of work. If it were simple, the entire neighborhood would all be millionaires, right? But in neighborhoods all across the country, most people are broke. I am not just referring to the poor areas or even the middle class. I am talking about the "rich" areas too.

Want to try something fun? Take a drive in your car[34] over to a neighborhood that is considered to be "wealthy." You know what I mean: the one where all the doctors, lawyers, and business owners live. Big houses. Nice cars outside or in the garages. You'll see Lexus, BMWs, Mercedes, expensive SUVs for the moms to take the kids everywhere in and oh... Teslas. Lots of Teslas!

It looks pretty impressive, right?

The sad story is that many of these families are living a very lavish lifestyle that is crippling their long-term financial health. The houses you are seeing have huge mortgages on them. Oftentimes

---

[34] The one that is a few years old and paid for!

they are "underwater," which means they owe more on the house than it is worth in the marketplace. Or maybe they have a tiny bit of equity[35], which in effect is not much different than renting.

There are many "Benzo Bobbies[36]" living in these neighborhoods. A common mantra among these people is "if I make more money I can buy more things!" You remember Dr. Paul from Chapter 4, right? People like him (and there are many) never make enough money. They sink further and further into a downward spiral. Those expenses keep going up, along with their stress level.

How do I know this? Because I have seen it all firsthand. Many of these people came to me begging for help. They were desperate. Once you get past the fancy cars, clothes, and castle-like homes and discover a person's true net worth, it becomes

---

[35] Home equity is essentially an estimate of what your home is worth minus what you owe.
[36] See chapter 11.

obvious that only a small percentage of people who look rich actually are.

You, on the other hand, will be rich. Better, you'll be at peace.

When you become the Neighborhood Millionaire, you will look back at your hard work and say "this was definitely worth it!" Don't give up the fight now. The first part of this book was about building the ground floor. The second part was about removing wrong choices and creating a firm foundation.

The third is about building a huge pile of money.

After you read Part Three, it will be tempting to jump straight into the tactics. Resist this desire if you haven't completed the first steps[37]. Follow the teachings exactly as laid out. If you start picking and choosing, making exceptions here and there, I

---

[37] Meaning you are regularly making goals, drawing up a budget, living within your means, are completely debt-free, and have 3-6 months of an emergency fund saved up.

guarantee this will not work. You will not become the Neighborhood Millionaire.

Stick to the plan, be tenacious, and follow along as if your life depends on this. Because, as it turns out, it does!

Before you turn the page, close your eyes and say out loud:

"I am becoming The Neighborhood Millionaire."

**You will be rich.
Better, you'll be at peace.**

The Future

Chapter 24 - From Average Wealth to Millionaire

At this point you have made and accomplished goals. You have built and followed a budget. You spend less money than you make every month. You have gotten yourself out of debt. You have a nice emergency fund set up of at least six months of expenses so when unexpected expenses come your way (and they will), you do not have to go back into debt.

First of all - congratulations! Being out of debt means you do not have monthly payments on ANYTHING with the exception of a home. That means at this point, you get to answer a very fun question. What should you do with all the extra money you have every month?

The answer to this question is: invest it.

Investing a portion of your income each and every month is the best way to build wealth and become the Neighborhood Millionaire. The earlier you begin, the better because you take advantage of compounding interest over time. As I've mentioned several times now, I do not want you to begin investing until you have systematically worked the steps I have outlined so far. It will be counterproductive. Investing your money when you have credit card debt and car payments simply makes no sense at all. So PLEASE follow the order here! If you have a financial planner who disagrees I would seriously consider finding a new one.[38]

Investing is the key activity that has made millionaires ever since there was a concept of millionaires. "Investing" is one of those words that sounds big and scary. This is partly because financial gurus overcomplicate what should be simple. Simply, investing is this: putting your money somewhere it can grow.

---

[38] Don't worry. We'll cover financial planners in a bit.

How much exactly should you invest every month? Great question. It depends how quickly you want to reach your goal and how extravagant you want your lifestyle to be. Generally speaking, the more you can invest, the quicker you can pile up cash for the long haul.

A good guideline is to sock away 15% of your income every month. Should you carve this number into your skin? Probably not. Are you going to die if you don't hit it? No. 15% is simply an ideal amount for the Neighborhood Millionaire. Much lower, and the road to millionaire-dom is long and slow. Much higher, and you won't get to enjoy any of the pleasures and comforts you worked so hard for! 15% is the sweet spot.

What's more important is that you commit to investing. If you do not do this, you will NEVER become wealthy, and that is a promise. It makes no difference how much money you make every month or every year. If you do not invest, you will not become the Neighborhood Millionaire. If you simply keep reading about it and procrastinating and waiting until you get it perfect, you are missing out on the two most important aspects - time and compounding interest.[39]

The rest of this book will cover the specifics of investing. If you've been living well below your means anyway, this should be easy. The beauty of investing is that instead of your cash (plus interest) going to the stupid credit card companies, both the cash AND the interest goes to your future self.

Before you turn the page, close your eyes and say out loud:

"I am becoming The Neighborhood Millionaire."

---

[39] We'll cover this in the next chapter.

Chapter 25 - Compound Interest: The Most Powerful Force in the Universe

It might sound extreme to call compound interest "the most powerful force in the universe." And it would be... if it wasn't for the person who claimed it to be true in the first place: Albert Einstein.

The genius went on to say "The person who understands it, earns it. And the person who doesn't, pays it!"

We can't discuss investing without compound interest. You must understand it and utilize it in your path to becoming the Neighborhood Millionaire." **Compound interest is the "quick start" and best kept secret for you to ultimately become the Neighborhood Millionaire.**

If you are under age 35, you have a tremendous advantage over anyone beginning later in life. But as

I have stated many times here, no matter how old you are, no matter how much you earn and no matter what mistakes you have made up until now, it is never too late to get started on this journey, so long as you start today!

Compound interest is any interest that is calculated on your initial investment[40] AND also on the accumulated interest from previous periods. With compound interest, you earn "interest on your interest."

Let me give you an example by showing three imaginary investors all on their quest to become the Neighborhood Millionaire.

Jeremy, a young man who wanted to get started early in life, was able to invest $1000 every month from the time he was 25 up until 35. Then life changed and he was not able to invest any more after age 35. He left his original investment intact so it continued

---

[40] That initial investment is called "the principle," by the way

to earn interest. Let's be super conservative and say his money earned an average of 7% up until his retirement age of 65.

Even though he didn't invest a single penny more than the $132,000 he'd scraped together over 11 years. On his 65th birthday, Jeremy had close to $1,500,000 in his investment account! He became the Neighborhood Millionaire with almost no effort!

Now meet Nathan. Nathan got a bit of a later start, but he invested the same $1000 every month from age 35 until 45. Like Jeremy, he stopped at that point and left his investment intact until retirement age.

When he turned 65, Nathan had $750,000 in his account. By starting ten years later, his ending balance was about half of what it would have been had he started at age 25, even with the same amount invested!

Finally, we have Remy. Remy was more of a free spirit early in life, but at age 45, she buckled down and began investing the same $1000 per month up until age 55. And just like the others, she stopped after ten years but left everything in the account until age 65. Can you guess what Remy's balance was at her retirement age of 65?

If you guessed about half of what Nathan had, you are correct! Remy had about $375,000 in her account. Now don't get me wrong, that is still a lot of money. It's a great amount, but imagine if she'd done that earlier in life. She could have still been the same free spirit dreamer throughout her 30s and 40s, except she would have had **four times more money** and would be the Neighborhood Millionaire!

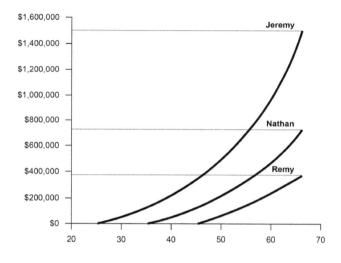

Remember, all three of them, Jeremy, Nathan and Remy, invested the exact same amount of money. It was $120,000 over ten years. They simply did it at different times in their lives.

This illustrates the power of compound interest.[41] The earlier you are able to start, the better the

---

[41] You might hear "compoundING" interest. It's the same thing.

benefits. If Jeremy was able to start at age 20 instead of age 25, and then stop ten years later at age 30, he would be a MULTI-millionaire by the time he reached 65 without ever doing anything else!

Again, I want to reemphasize that no matter where you are in life now and whatever you have done in the past, it is NEVER too late to get started reaching Neighborhood Millionaire status. Otherwise what are your choices? If you do nothing, I guarantee that you will not get there.

Before you turn the page, close your eyes and say out loud:

"I am becoming The Neighborhood Millionaire."

Chapter 26 - Starter Accounts: Investing for "Retirement"

What should you invest your money in? This is the age old question.

There are so many possibilities. It is extremely complex and totally requires at least four academic degrees to understand thoroughly. At least... all that is what the gurus say.

Maybe that's why volumes and volumes of books have been written on this topic and Americans are more confused and more broke than ever. The truth is the gurus lied. Investing is only as complex as you want it to be. Let's try the simple way first.

Before jumping into specific investments, there is a more important principle that you need to understand: before-tax investments and after-tax investments. Before-tax investments are exactly what they sound like. These opportunities allow you to set aside a portion of your money to start working for you *before* paying taxes on them.

This is good news, considering most Americans pay an average of $15,322 in taxes[42] every year. Wouldn't it be nice to keep at least some of that money for yourself?

After-tax investments are, again, exactly what they seem. You invest the money AFTER you have already been taxed on it! Your investment grows, but you will still have to pay taxes on the gains once you cash them out.

What type of investment do you think is better? If you answered "before tax" investments, you are correct. We try to maximize our before tax investments.

The most common forms of before-tax investments are retirement plans. You have likely heard of these.

---

[42] According to 2018 IRS data.

When someone mentions an IRA or a 401(k), they are referencing retirement plans. An IRA (Individual Retirement Account) is an account you can set up and manage on your own[43], and a 401(k) is a retirement plan through your place of employment. There are other types as well, but these are the two most common. Please remember that neither an IRA nor a 401(k) is an investment. Think of it as a special "container" that holds your investment(s).

You are free to choose which types of investment go into your IRA. Normally your employer manages the company 401(k). The most common investment for an IRA is mutual funds. But some people put single stocks into their IRA and others put real estate, gold, or silver.

To go a tiny bit deeper, there are two types of IRAs and 401(k)s - traditional and ROTH. Traditional means that you deduct your investment at the time of your deposit, and you end up paying taxes later

---

[43] The name tells you this: "Individual Retirement Account."

when you pull the money out. You will pay taxes on everything, the principle and the money you have made (your gains).

A ROTH is pretty much the opposite. You pay taxes on the initial investment now, and then your money grows totally tax free. So yes, you are probably thinking that a ROTH is not actually a before tax investment. And you are absolutely correct. But the fact that you get tax free growth is what's so cool about the ROTH IRA or ROTH 401(k).

Which is better, ROTH or traditional? Again, I love simplicity. The nuanced and complicated answer is: "it depends." But the rule Neighborhood Millionaires follow is to first maximize the amount of money you put into your ROTH IRAs and your ROTH 401(k).[44]

Invest the most you can in your retirement account(s) every year up to the legal limits. The IRA

---

[44] The 401(k) maximum is up to your employer and out of your control, but invest as much as you can.

limits are always changing, but a quick Google search will tell you what's possible.[45] Do the same with your 401(k) if you are fortunate enough to have one through your work. Some employers are able to match your 401(k) deposit up to a certain percentage. Although they call it a match, I call it "free money." If it is offered, take advantage of it!

Are you married? That means both you and your spouse can EACH have your own retirement accounts in your names which for the most part will DOUBLE the amount your household can invest your pre-tax dollars.

To sum up, IRAs and 401(k)s are long term investment plans that have huge tax advantages and are designed to supply you with an income upon retirement. If you do this right, you could have millions of dollars in your accounts at retirement, even if you make a modest income now. How would that feel? I will tell you it feels pretty damn good!

---

[45] Search for "maximum amount I can deposit into my IRA in (year)."

I want to be clear here. You don't have to "retire" in order to take money out of your retirement funds. You simply have to be a certain age.[46] Even if you plan to work on passion projects forever (like me), it's nice to have a big, fat nest egg while you do.

Big picture, you want to put as much of your money as possible into retirement plans every year. And remember, all you're doing is dropping money into a container. Once the money is in the container, you can allocate it to different investments.

What types of investments are best? We'll talk about that in the next chapter.

For now, before you turn the page, close your eyes and say out loud:

"I am becoming The Neighborhood Millionaire."

---

[46] 59.5 years old, in case you were wondering.

Chapter 27 - Stay Stress-Free with the S&P

After the retirement containers are filled up, what should you invest them in?[47]

Sadly, 401(k) plans (similar retirement programs) are typically managed by an employer. That means you are likely at their mercy as far as what you can invest in. You can only dump money in, and they manage it. However, if you are investing on your own, you can allocate that money wherever you want.

This road to freedom is filled with potholes, though.

There are a plethora of places to put your money out there that catch unwary investors every day: single stocks, gold, Bitcoin, junk bonds, municipal

---

[47] Once more - I only recommend investing your money once you have a monthly budget that works, a complete freedom from debt except for your primary home, and an emergency fund of 6-12 months of living expenses. Please donot deviate from this strategy as it will hurt you. I promise. This is the last time I'll mention it... probably.

bonds and certificates of deposits to name just a few. It's nuts out there and most people are all over the place. Thanks to the lack of focus, these people never achieve true wealth or reach their goals.

Before you become a Neighborhood Millionaire, I'd advise you stick with the investment that is not only the absolute easiest and simplest investment, but also happens to be the one that will likely give you the most consistent returns over time.

It's called the S&P 500.

When you hear people say that "the stock market is doing well" or "the stock market had a terrible day today," they are probably referring to the S&P 500 Index or more simply, "the S&P." S&P stands for "Standard and Poor's." This is essentially a group of the 500 largest publicly-traded companies in the United States. So, the S&P 500 Index basically measures how the "stock market" is doing. It's as simple as that.

In this case, simple does quite well over time.

The average annualized total return for the S&P 500 index over the past 90 years is 9.8% percent. That means if you had put $100 in the stock market 90 years ago, it would now be worth $451,000. Of course it varies year to year. That's why we're using an average.

Now, I can already hear it. So many hotshots will be saying that I have no idea what I am talking about and that an average return of 9.8% is not really that good. These geniuses will tell you not to invest in The S&P.

"Buy Apple stock and you will become wealthy."

"My cousin made a fortune from Tesla stock."

"I have a great tip for you about a company that's going public…"

Please IGNORE all of these people.

Do some people make a ton of money from single stocks? Sure. You'll hear about them occasionally. What you don't hear about so often are the millions of people who lose money or go completely broke because they picked wrong.

Back in the old days, I made a LOT of money by investing in Intel and Microsoft. That happened by sheer dumb luck. I would NEVER try that again now, and I certainly wouldn't advise anyone else to do so. Next time I may not be so lucky.

No, you will not get rich quick[48] by investing in the S&P 500. But Neighborhood Millionaires aren't worried about that. We are steady and smart. We avoid stupid mistakes, knowing that patience pays off.

---

[48] By the way, there is no predictable way to get rich quickly, no matter what your friends say. The most likely result of trying to do so is financial disaster.

If you had put $100 in the stock market 90 years ago, it would now be worth $451,000.

How do you invest your money in the S&P? It's pretty darn simple. You put it in an "index fund." An index fund is a mutual fund[49] that mirrors a particular index. In our case we will pick a fund that mirrors the S&P 500. When the S&P goes up, your index fund will go up. And same for when it goes down. You do not have to buy 500 individual stocks and manage them all. It's all done for you in one simple transaction.

You can make investing more complicated than that. But why would you want to?

---

[49] A fund made up of a group of stocks.

Before you turn the page, close your eyes and say out loud:

"I am becoming The Neighborhood Millionaire."

Chapter 28 - Setting Up Your First Fund

There are many ways to open up any sort of investment fund. One common way is to use a financial planner. However, there are many obstacles in the way of finding a "good" planner who won't screw you over, so first, I will share exactly how I set up my account with no outside help.

Whether you are setting up an index fund, a Traditional IRA, a ROTH IRA, or some other account, your best bet is to use any of the online brokerage accounts such as e-Trade, Vanguard, Fidelity, or Charles Schwab.[50]

I have an account with eTrade that I've held for decades. (When I find something that works well, I

---

[50] I have no affiliation with any of these platforms. I am simply sharing what I do and what has been very successful for me. There are many online brokerage houses and you are free to use whichever you like.

stick with it). You can do the same by going online to us.etrade.com. Then click "Open an account."

Once you have opened your account, you will need to send in some money. Follow the on-screen instructions to do this.

When you have cash in your eTrade account, it's time to invest. Now you can invest in any stock or mutual fund through eTrade. Do not be tempted to outthink common sense. Keep it simple. I invest mostly in "VTSAX," which is Vanguard Total Stock Market Index Fund.

Simply follow the instructions in your newly opened eTrade account to buy VTSAX. If you ever hit a roadblock they also have very good customer service. After that, all you have to do is let the money grow.

You're done. You're investing. Crazy, right? By reading paragraphs, you're in!

By the way, I want to point out that when I say "let the money grow," I don't mean "obsessively check your number every single day to see what is happening." That's what I did early in my investing, and let me assure you it is a path to impatience, anxiety, and annoyance. I'll go ahead and spoil the drama by telling you what will happen to your money over the next few years.

There are days where the market will go up and there are days that it will go down. There will be days where your money looks like it will plummet to the ground, only to bounce back up. There will be global crises, national issues, and local fears. There will be whole years when you will be down or make very little. And there will be years when you will make a lot.

You control none of this. You only control whether or not you invest. Do that, and do not obsess. If history is any indicator, your investments will go up over time to the tune of 10% per year on average. I believe that the U.S. economy is strong and will not fail. Sure, there could be a one to two year bear market at some point, but the bull markets[51] have always won out over time. And that means you will.

Remember, the order of these steps is important. If you need short term money for something, please do not invest it in the market.

For example, if you are saving up for a down payment for a house and you think it will be in the next year or two where you will need it, keep that money in something safe such as a bank savings account, even though it won't be earning interest. Why? Because if you do invest that money, there is always a chance the market could be down when you need to pull it out, and then you are screwed! Not only that, but if you're pulling funds out of a retirement account before you are retirement age, you'll get punched in the face with a huge penalty as well as a tax bill.

---

[51] For simplicity's sake, a "bear market" is when stocks go down and a "bull market" is when they go up.

Invest money you don't need right away. Then, leave it alone. That little seed will grow into an enormous tree of financial freedom. It really is that simple. Anyone who tells you otherwise is selling you something. And trust me, there are plenty of people doing that...

Before we talk about them though, and before you turn the page, close your eyes and say out loud:

"I am becoming The Neighborhood Millionaire."

Chapter 29 - Real Estate, Bitcoin, and Beyond

The point of this book is to give simple, foolproof advice. That's exactly what you've read up to this point.

Still, with all the lies and half-truths floating around out there, I want to talk about a few sexy areas of money that I *haven't* recommended in this book. There are, in fact, other investments you could make beside the S&P that may make you wealthy. The problem is most of those require a level of risk that can only be avoided with an enormous amount of specific education - education the average person does not have much time for.

One such investment is real estate. It's true that many people have made a lot of money - millions and billions - in real estate. There are actually rumors that you *can't* become a millionaire without real estate.

It's not true.

Other than my residential homes, I have invested exactly $0 in real estate. Just like you, I personally know people who own real estate and claim to be doing very well with it. Just like you, I've been intrigued by the idea of income properties. Just like you, I've been preached to about the importance of "diversification."[52]

At one point, I had a plan to find a little single family home here in Salt Lake City, pay cash for it, fix up what was necessary, find a good tenant, and then watch the money start to roll in. I found a knowledgeable real estate guy in the area who was helping me narrow down my search.

---

[52] Usually by people who were broke to begin with.

In the end, I decided not to do it. The reason is very simple. Let me explain.

Every investment decision I make is based on two rules:

Do I understand this investment?
Would this money do better elsewhere?

When I say "understand" an investment, I mean I need to PERFECTLY clear what it is I am putting my money in. Even though I have never owned an investment property, I did quite a bit of reading about real estate as an investment. I knew about how much an investment property would cost me. I learned that there are really only three ways that properties can make you money.[53] And I knew approximately how much I could get in rent every month. I worked the numbers and I worked them hard.

---

[53] The three ways are rental income, appreciation (if the property actually goes up in value), and tax benefits.

But as much as I crunched the numbers, I could not justify buying a home as an investment. Not only would it be a lot of work, but it seemed as though I could do better in the S&P 500.

I called my real estate guy and told him I'm out. That afternoon I put all of the money I was going to put in the new home into the S&P 500 instead. Less than a year later, that money has made me $158,146.52. Not too bad. right?

Real estate, especially in the internet era, is marketed as one of the sexiest investments you can make. These messages are filled with terms like "no money down" and "passive income." Trust me. Real estate is hardly that. Owning and managing properties takes cash, is a LOT of work and filled with potential problems. Could you make a lot of money? Sure. But the road to real estate riches is rarely as glamorous as it seems.

Speaking of glamour, let's talk about Bitcoin and cryptocurrency.

I invested in Bitcoin and some other cryptocurrencies a few years ago. It seemed like an interesting concept, and had the money to do so. I did not invest anything that I could not afford to lose. Have I made money in Bitcoin? The answer is yes. But it is a very risky and volatile investment that I do not recommend to anyone who is attempting to become the Neighborhood Millionaire. So unless you have a net worth of well above one million dollars, my advice is to stay away.

The road to the village of Neighborhood Millionaires is paved with slow, smart, safe decisions made consistently over time. People who find fast fortunes usually watch them drain as quickly as they come.

Before you turn the page, close your eyes and say out loud:

"I am becoming The Neighborhood Millionaire."

Chapter 30 - A Financial Planner is Not a Magic Solution

Okay. Let's slow down. There have been a lot of acronyms in these last chapters. There has also been math. If you hate those things, you may be tempted to start the hunt for a financial planner to make it all go away.

This is the worst reason to look for a financial planner.

You need to be fully informed and aware of every single decision you make regarding your money. That is why you are reading this book. A financial planner should act as an additional teacher - someone who can answer your questions and guide you when you need to be guided. He is NOT someone you just turn your finances over to and say "you take care of this and make me wealthy because I do not want to be involved!"

Whether or not to hire a financial planner is a complex topic that I will make as simple as possible. The short answer is yes. It is a good idea to have a planner that understands personal finance as well as your situation to guide you and your family along the path to becoming wealthy.

The long answer involves a flashy office, a guy named Barry, and something called "private placements..."

Honestly, I have been screwed so many times in my life that it's surprising I have any money left at all. I have used financial planners during my life and continue to do so. I have a great one now, but I believe that I have seen the good, the bad, the ugly and the VERY UGLY. The one disaster I have the most nightmares about, though, is a man I've come to call Hurricane Barry.

I met Barry through a very wealthy "friend." At the time Barry and I met, I had just crossed the million-dollar mark in my net worth. I was eager (a little *too* eager) to turn that million dollars into multi-millions. Barry seemed like the perfect guy to make that happen. And I will admit that our relationship was perfect for a while. Well... perfect for Barry.

Hurricane Barry saw how much money I had worked hard to save. He saw pretty quickly that I didn't have enough knowledge to know when he was blowing hot air. He also saw a vision of *my* money coming to *his* account in the form of commissions. Barry quickly smooth-talked me into buying a few "private placement" investments that were a "sure bet" for making some really big money.[54]

I trusted Barry and handed him the keys to the vault. And Barry did what he did best: scammed an ignorant man out of his money. Barry was incredibly

---

[54] What I know now, but didn't know then, is that private placements actually do have a large potential upside, but they are also insanely risky. More times than not, you'll lose everything.

efficient. Exactly a year later, I'd lost my millionaire status. Barry had a big chunk of my money thanks to his huge fees and I lost the rest of it due to a "market correction." Guess what I learned during this time? Private placements do not rebound when the stock market does. When they go to zero (as mine did), you are flat busted. Almost a third of my net worth was gone in the blink of an eye.

Barry disappeared soon after this. He was on to the next victim.

> **You need to be fully informed and aware of every single decision you make regarding your money.**

Barry and people like him are always very charming. A similar "financial wizard" conned his way into my parents' hearts and ripped them off for decades. I'm not sure what he did with all the money, but some of it went to lavish parties that he threw for his clients. Don't worry, he always told everyone goodbye afterwards... through the window of his limo.

I tell this story about Barry, and the other story about my parents, because I want to warn you, not scare you. You cannot be too careful when it comes to finding a financial planner. Certainly you want to talk to your friends and family to see who they trust, but you also want to be armed with information of your own.

I actually have a few more horror stories which I don't even need to get into right now. One of them actually involves investing in ships in the middle of the ocean. It was recommended by a very "reputable" financial planner. A friend of mine. Sounds fine, right? Well every single one of those

189

ships SUNK! Maybe my next book should be about all of the stupid things I have done that resulted in big losses. Would you read it?

Let's stay on track for now. It's helpful to have a series of questions to test any financial planner you speak with. Luckily for you, that's exactly what you'll get in the next chapter.

But before we go there, close your eyes and say out loud:

"I am becoming The Neighborhood Millionaire."

Chapter 31 - Three Questions to Keep You From Getting Conned

There are many different types of financial planners, but as far as I am concerned, there is only ONE TYPE that is acceptable. That one type is a "fee only" planner who is a "fiduciary."

Before we get into the three questions, let's break down these terms.

A "fee only" planner means exactly what it sounds like. Your planner is giving you advice, and you are paying him or her for their time, the same way you would with a lawyer, an accountant, a plumber, or an electrician. They are performing a service for you, and in return you pay them for that service. That service is financial advice! Nothing else.

A "fiduciary" by definition is a financial planner who is legally obligated to act in your best interest. There can be no ulterior motive such as selling you a product that they will profit from.

Now this must seem crazy. "Dr. Dave, you mean that there are actually financial planners who do *not* have to act in your best interest?" Unfortunately the answer is yes, there are. You MUST stay away from these types!

In order to do that, you need to navigate the lies they will tell. There are three great questions to ask a prospective advisor to find out if he or she is truly a fiduciary.

Question #1: Are you a fiduciary?

This is a simple question, and of course the answer needs to be "YES!" However, the problem is that there are some slimy planners[55] out there who will lie right to your face. So even a "yes" is not necessarily 100% safe.

A couple of years ago I took my mom to see some guy that advertised heavily on the radio preaching

---

[55] (and I use the word planner very loosely)

that he could guarantee a nice income to the listeners for the rest of their lives, giving them peace of mind in retirement.

Every red flag went off at that moment inside my head. I told mom to stay away, but of course my mom insisted that he was a good advisor because he had his own radio show.[56]

My mom got sucked in and scheduled an appointment. I told her that I wanted to come along because I knew what questions to ask the guy.

He had a nice little office space in a high rise building in a suburb of Baltimore. We walked in, and after a little lightweight chit chat with a side of stale coffee, I asked him if he was a fiduciary. He looked me right in the eye and said "yes."

As it turned out, though, the one "wonderful" product he recommended was a crappy annuity that

---

[56] Surely they wouldn't give a radio show to just anyone. Right? Right??????

would tie up all of my mom's money forever, give her a mediocre rate of return and would have been a heavily loaded commission on the front end to line this guy's pockets to boot.

Does that sound like he was acting in my mother's "best interest?" I didn't think so either. He was no fiduciary. He was a salesman. I politely told my mom that we were not doing business with the guy.

Question #2: Are you always legally bound to act in my best interest?

Again, this answer has to be "YES!" But again, there are a lot of snakes out there.

When you ask this question, I would get the potential planner to put in writing in those exact words: "I am legally bound to act in your best interest." Then ask him/her to sign below those words and keep the page for your records! Nobody wants a court battle. But nobody wants to have their entire savings drained by fake financial planners either.

Question #3: How do you get paid?
The only acceptable answer would be that YOU (the client) pay him for his time or he gets a percentage of your assets that he manages for you. Typically that number is around 1%.

If he starts hemming and hawing and says things like "don't worry, you don't need to pay me," or something like "I get paid by the brokerage house," this is a big red flag. Why? Because it means he is making a commission on products that he is going to sell you. Run (don't walk) to the nearest door! You need someone who is 100% unbiased and working only on your behalf. But remember, all of the salesmen will stretch the truth and say of course they have your interest at heart. Be super careful. Take your time and make a good choice. Don't let anyone push you into a decision.

The right person may be hard to find, but they will be worth their weight in gold (sometimes literally). What should that right person do for you? Great question. For starters, he or she can guide you to the right type of investments for you as well as the proper allocation based on your risk tolerance, age, and target retirement age.

You'll also get an insider's look into the taxes involved with every choice you make. I keep a financial planner around mostly for the tax advice. I use a good accountant as well - always a CPA (Certified Public Accountant). Since I am not a tax expert and the tax laws are always changing, I need someone to help! I don't know what I don't know, and "I've never heard of that law" is NOT an excuse the IRS likes to hear.[57] One good strategy tip a year

---

[57] Here is a quick example of tax consequences most nice people get caught by. If you want to give someone a nice expensive gift or some cash? Well that's really nice of you. Just make sure you read up and understand about the "gift tax" that you may incur!

from my guy will much more than pay for me to keep him on for the following year.

A good financial planner can also help to talk you "off the cliff," to coin a phrase. Too often we foresee a crazy political event, a pandemic, or maybe a recession coming up and we start to panic and decide to SELL all of our investments immediately because of course the world is coming to an end. This would almost always be a tremendous mistake made by inexperienced investors. Your financial planner will talk some sense into you before you make a deadly move such as that.

More importantly than those things though, a good financial guide can discuss your goals with you and then lay out a proper plan to help you get there. The right planner will always be more interested in *your* future, not theirs. They should ask you where you're planning to go and what you're planning to do as you get older.

Can you do it all yourself? Of course. Especially if you absorb the lessons in this book. Remember, you can't just turn over all your money and hope for the best anyway! You are responsible for every decision in your life. A good financial planner can simply help you make better ones.

Before you turn the page, close your eyes and say out loud:

"I am becoming The Neighborhood Millionaire."

Chapter 32 - The Only Three Things You Can Do With Money

We've spent a lot of time in the mud here, talking about the ins and outs of money. The details. The grit. But as we wind this book down, I want to pull back a little bit and take a broader, philosophical look at the purpose of money.

There are really only three things you can do with money:

- Spend it
- Invest (save) it
- Give it away

I have found that the best way to live is to do a combination of all three.

Spending:
The Neighborhood Millionaire is not flashy. As I have said, we do not drive the flashy expensive cars that attract attention at the stop lights. We can if we

like, but there is really no reason to. We generally do not wear the most expensive designer clothes, nor do we sport fancy jewelry.

We do spend money at times because that is what it's for. My advice for once you become the Neighborhood Millionaire is to be very humble and do not buy things to impress others. Buy things that you truly want, things that will enhance your life. A few years ago, my wife and I bought a nice RV motorhome. We paid cash of course. We absolutely love it as we travel around the country, making any mountain, desert, river or ocean our backyard for a night or for a month. It's truly wonderful. I would say it was one of the most fun purchases of my life.

Investing:
I don't need to talk about investing much more here because it's covered in previous chapters. Investing is the vehicle that will turn you into the Neighborhood Millionaire. Never forget that. Never stop investing. The only exception is when you get

to the point where you are retired and you are then using your investments to live on!

Giving:
There is nothing more powerful than helping others. There are many ways to give and many causes to give to. I encourage you to give to the people, organizations, churches, synagogues that you feel connected to.

Being huge animal lovers, Yoko and I give a lot of our money to organizations that help animals. Our primary reason for giving is to help others. We do not expect anything in return, but I will say that somehow the universe works in very mysterious ways. Practically every single time I give, either money comes back to me in some way or something extremely positive happens in my life. I do not think this is a coincidence. I have heard this from a huge number of people over the years who say the same thing.

There were times when things were tough and it was not so easy for me to write checks to charitable organizations. But I did so anyway. That's how important giving was and is for me. The Neighborhood Millionaire gives from the heart and does not expect anything in return.

Balance between these three options is key. Remember that as you climb to the Neighborhood Millionaire mountaintop, and never forget it once you're there.

Before you turn the page, close your eyes and say out loud:

"I am becoming The Neighborhood Millionaire."

Final Thoughts

Why do people try to make personal finance so damn complicated?

I am always amazed at what lengths and what crazy schemes people will go to in pursuit of wealth. They take advice from broke people and think it will work. They take ridiculous stock tips. They buy real estate on credit. They buy and sell based on hunches. They panic.

Oh my God it's so crazy out there. But I guess if it were simple, no one would need a book such as this. The reason I wrote this book is to teach you that there are no crazy, esoteric strategies that you need to figure out before you can become a millionaire. The techniques are actually quite simple. And... they work! If you follow all the simple principles I've laid out in this book, there is absolutely no doubt in my mind that you will become the Neighborhood Millionaire.

But please understand. You can't just "pick and choose" the strategies that are appealing to you. You can't do this halfway. There is no such thing as being "millionaire-ish!" You must be all in to truly become the Neighborhood Millionaire.

Nowhere in this book have I said this is an easy process. But as you travel along this journey, you will discover that a difficult start turns into an incredible finish. Every step you take will make you feel more and more excited. Each day you will see yourself getting closer and closer to your goal.

Just think of what it will feel like when you become the Neighborhood Millionaire. You will have an air of confidence that comes from the ability to do anything you want. Better, you won't even have to live lavishly because you will be so happy in your life that you do not have to "prove" to anyone that you have money!

You can certainly keep living the way you have been living so far and doing things the same way. Or you can take on this way of life. It's your choice.

But, you picked this book up and you have read this far. That means you are definitely on your way. Again, it does not matter how old you are or how you have lived your life so far. You have it in you to get this done! I know you are going to do it, and sometime soon you will join the elite group of Neighborhood Millionaires!

So congratulations to my future "Neighborhood Millionaire!" Now, before you put the book down, close your eyes and say this out loud for a final time:

"I have become The Neighborhood Millionaire."

Now That You've Finished...

I am going to highly recommend you do three things that will greatly increase your chances of becoming the Neighborhood Millionaire.

Firstly, you may put the book down for now, but please keep it close by. Read it at least once every two or three months. More often if you can. Mark it up as much as you like and make sure you read your highlights at the very least! By doing this, the principles will be firmly planted in your mind and you will have a much better chance of succeeding in becoming the Neighborhood Millionaire.

Secondly, please feel free to share a link to purchasing this book with one of your very close friends or family members. Not only will you be helping one more person achieve the Neighborhood Millionaire status, but you will also have someone with whom you can engage in meaningful conversation and discussion about becoming the Neighborhood Millionaire. You can hold each other accountable and both of you will likely reach millionaire status even sooner than if you went at it alone!

Thirdly, please sign up for my free newsletter by going to **join.davidmadow.com**. It's called "Dave Discovers" and each issue is full of great practical advice and tips that will help you live the life of your dreams.

Welcome to the world of being the Neighborhood Millionaire.

Acknowledgements

I would like to thank my wife Yoko for all of her support that she gave me while writing this book. Again, I cannot overemphasize how important it is for you to have a partner who is on the same page as you are.

I would also like to thank my children as well as their spouses. Lauren, Michael, Keria and Evan, I love you all! And my grandchildren, Jeremy, Nate and Remy! Even though we are geographically not so close to each other, you guys are always in my heart.

To my Mom, Zesa Lois, and my brothers Marshall and Richard, along with our Dad, Selvin. (May he rest in peace). And of course my family in Japan, Takemitsu, Reiko and Tatsuya. I could not have done this without all of you!

About David Madow

David Madow is an American dentist, entrepreneur, public speaker, author and video content creator. After graduating from The Baltimore College of Dental Surgery, Dr. Madow completed a one-year general practice residency, built a dental practice from scratch, and later sold it to pursue other business interests.

In 1989, David and his brother Richard started a business with nothing but a big idea, a small kitchen table, and a rickety pickup truck. Their little dream turned into The Madow Center for Dental Practice Success, which grew into a seven-figure business. For over thirty years David and Richard have been key opinion leaders in dentistry, speaking to audiences of thousands all across North America. For the past fifteen years they have both been featured on the cover of "Dentistry Today" as leaders in dental education.

David made nearly every financial mistake a person could make along the way, causing him to develop a fierce passion for goal setting and personal finance. Ultimately, he discovered a predictable way to true financial freedom. That path became this book – *The Neighborhood Millionaire.*

Dr. Dave loves the outdoors. He is an avid skier, slow runner, and consistent hiker. He and his wife live in Utah

One More Thing...

Will you do me a small favor?

Head over to Amazon and leave a review for this book. Amazon reviews are far and away the best currency a little book like this can collect. It only costs you two minutes, and you are literally changing the world when you make it happen.

Thanks in advance,

- Dr. Dave